UNITED TO CHRIST

A THEOLOGY OF HOPE AND GLORY

DAVID L. PARKER

Independently published

© 2020 David L. Parker. All rights reserved.

Scripture quotations taken from the New American Standard Bible®, Copyright © 1960, 1962, 1963, 1968, 1971, 1972, 1973, 1975, 1977, 1995 by The Lockman Foundation. Used by permission. www.Lockman.org

ISBN: 979-8-6694-2049-9

Printed in the United States of America

This book is printed on acid-free paper.

First Edition

...Christ in you, the hope of glory.

- Colossians 1:27

For Tobie, Megan and David, Will and Kayla, and John who are wondrously united to Christ.

Table of Contents

Table of Contents Continued

Introduction

Union with Christ is the central truth of Christianity.

Scripture teaches us that every believer is graciously united to Christ the Savior. God imparts Himself to us in Christ, filling us and blessing us by His Spirit, and forever possessing us as His own chosen and beloved people. In this wondrous union, we are truly interpenetrated and energized by the Spirit of Christ, yet we maintain our own individuality and personal distinctness.

Union with Christ is union with a personal, risen, living, omnipresent Savior. It is a union of everlasting life.

In this union, all of the debt and liabilities of man are assumed by Christ in His saving work on the cross. In this union, Christ's righteousness, blessings, honor, glory and power are shared with those united to Him through faith.

Every Christian has entered into exactly such a union as this. Our Union with Christ may seem to us to be only an external bond, but it is an inward and spiritual bond that makes us forever His own special possession and He ours.

The mystery made known by the gospel is *"Christ in you the hope of glory"*. Oftentimes, we only grasp this when we are seeking some closer association to a Savior who we think is external to us. Trying to find this closer walk, we are thrilled to learn that we already have a bond with Christ that is deeper, livelier and more amazing than we ever imagined.

The aim of this book is for you to grasp how intimate a union you have with Christ. When this union is understood, it becomes a beacon that will guide you into an abundant life marked by holiness, satisfaction and delighting in the Savior.

This book will examine your Union with Christ and show how this union changes your identity and animates your life.

Perhaps you have you been told that you are one with Christ. How are you one with Him? Does being one with Christ mean that you try to be one in mind, heart, or purpose with Him? Is being one with Christ a state that you aspire to?

Maybe you have been taught that Christ now lives in your heart. What does that really mean? Is it like saying the memory of a departed loved one lives always in your heart?

It is likely that you have read that you are in Christ. What exactly does this imply? Does this mean that you have been baptized? Does this mean that you attend church?

In this book, we will rely on the careful and prayerful study of Scripture to answer these questions. You will be blessed by the hope and glory found in Union with Christ.

This book is loosely based on Augustus Strong's Systematic Theology. Strong's brief treatment on Union with Christ inspired much of the outline and thought in this book.

This book is an expansion of chapter sixty-five from my summary of doctrine, Strong Faith. What I outlined there in two pages will be explored here over the next one hundred.

This book is intended for personal study and devotion. Each chapter is meant to be a clear, concise and illuminating explanation of Union with Christ that is easy to understand.

I pray that this book will help you to see and cherish your Union with Christ and deepen your communion with Him. May you henceforth confidently and joyfully proclaim: *"I am my beloved's, and his desire is for me"* (Song. 7:10).

Gain Christ! (Philippians 3:8)

David L. Parker

Mount Dora, FL

I. FIGURATIVE SCRIPTURAL REPRESENTATIONS OF UNION WITH CHRIST

Chapter 1

Union of a building and its foundation

The figure of a building and its foundation illustrates our rest in Christ and our fixed connection to Him.

- We are grounded in Christ as our foundation.
- We are living stones in Christ's temple.
- We thus furnish a habitation for God through Christ.

Our union with Christ is illustrated in Scripture with the union of a building and its foundation.

In ancient times, buildings were constructed on a large stone set at the structure's corner. This cornerstone was carefully selected for the foundation and alignment of the whole building. The cornerstone's strength and fitness were pivotal as all the other stones would rest on and connect to it.

In Isaiah 28:16, the prophet says that Father will send Christ to be "...*a tested stone, a costly cornerstone for the foundation, firmly placed.*" Because Christ is "*firmly placed*", those connected to Him find rest and establishment.

Our soul therefore finds its one true foundation in Christ. Psalms 118:22 says "*The stone which the builders rejected has become the chief corner stone.*"

Because Christ is our chief cornerstone, we are "...*being built up in Him...*" (Col. 2:7). We are built upon Him and are therefore in permanent connection to Him. It is through this divine connection that we become a dwelling place of God.

Ephesians 2:20-22 speaks of believers as *"having been built on the foundation of the apostles and prophets, Christ Jesus Himself being the corner stone, in whom the whole building, being fitted together, is growing into a holy temple in the Lord, in whom you also are being built together into a dwelling of God in the Spirit."*

> *Therefore thus says the Lord God, "Behold, I am laying in Zion a stone, a tested stone, a costly cornerstone for the foundation, firmly placed. He who believes in it will not be disturbed.*
> **–Isaiah 28:16**

In this passage we read that God Himself has expertly *"fitted together"* believers to Christ to be a living and growing *"dwelling of God"* for His own habitation. Here, we see the Trinity engaged in the establishment of our sweet repose in Christ and our permanent connection to Him.

In this passage, *"foundation"* is best translated as "belonging to the foundation". We are so precisely fitted to Christ according to God's perfect design and construction, that our union with Christ is indestructible. Nothing can separate us from Christ (Rom. 8:38-39). We belong to Him!

But we must come to Him. Jesus says *"Come to Me, all who are weary and heavy-laden, and I will give you rest"* (Matthew 11:28). When we come to Christ we find rest and acceptance in Him who *"...is choice and precious in the sight of God..."*, and thus resting in God's delight we *"... as living stones, are being built up as a spiritual house for a holy priesthood, to offer up spiritual sacrifices acceptable to God through Jesus Christ"* (1 Peter 2:4-5).

Bible verses for devotion:

Acts 4:10-12 –In Whom do we find salvation?

Jn. 10:27-30 – Who ensures our permanent ground?

Chapter 2

Union between Husband and Wife

The figure of marriage illustrates the steadfast love that forever joins the church to Christ and that makes us legally and organically one with Him.

- We are perfectly loved by Christ who gave Himself for us.
- We are separated unto and joined to Christ as His bride.
- We have present blessings and future hope in Christ.

The Old Testament often portrays God's people as married to God. The Song of Songs is a beautiful illustration of this love. It is allegorical poem that describes the union of Yahweh and His people under the figure of marriage. It illustrates God's intimate relationship with His people.

The picture of marriage is sometimes used in the Old Testament to comfort God's people and remind them of their special relationship with God. For example, Isaiah 54:5 says *"For your husband is your Maker, whose name is the LORD of hosts...."*

Other times, the figure of marriage is used in the Old Testament to call God's people back to Himself. Jeremiah 3:20 states *""Surely, as a woman treacherously departs from her lover, so you have dealt treacherously with Me, O house of Israel," declares the LORD."*

In the New Testament, Paul adopts the Old Testament illustration of marriage and applies it more precisely to the union of Christ with His beloved bride, the church. Marriage was given to prefigure Christ's union with us (Eph. 5:31-32).

In Rom. 7:4, Paul says *"Therefore, my brethren, you also were made to die to the Law through the body of Christ, so that you might be joined to another, to Him who was raised from the dead, in order that we might bear fruit for God."*

> *For this reason a man shall leave his father and mother and shall be joined to his wife, and the two shall become one flesh. This mystery is great; but I am speaking with reference to Christ and the church.*
> **—Ephesians 5:31-32**

Here we see under the figure of marriage that we are legally and organically one with Christ. United to Christ in His death, the church is wed to Christ and shares His legal standing and rights. United to Christ in His resurrection, the church is espoused to Christ as belonging to Him, receiving from Him and living for Him.

All of this is accomplished *"through the body of Christ"* to show us how profound the intimacy is between Christ and those *"joined"* to Him. He is presently joined so closely to us that there is no distance between us, though we see Him not.

The figure of marriage also looks forward to our glorious destiny. Revelation 19:7-8 says *""Let us rejoice and be glad and give the glory to Him, for the marriage of the Lamb has come and His bride has made herself ready." It was given to her to clothe herself in fine linen, bright and clean...."*

The church looks forward in blessed hope to celebrating the marriage supper of the Lamb. We look forward to being presented before Christ as His bride. As the bride of Christ, we expectantly say with the Spirit, *"Come"* (Rev. 22:17).

Bible verses for devotion:

Hosea 2:19-20 —How humbling is it to consider that the everlasting God establishes an eternal union with us!

Chapter 3

Union between the Vine and its Branches

The figure of the Vine and its branches illustrates the vital relationship in which we depend wholly on Christ for life and fruitfulness.

- We find continuous impartation of life from Christ.
- We find a new likeness of nature from this imparted life.
- We find fruitfulness only in connection with Christ.

In the Old Testament, the figure of the vine is used to depict Israel. For example, Psalms 80:8-9 says *"You removed a vine from Egypt; You drove out the nations and planted it. You cleared the ground before it, and it took deep root and filled the land."*

The prophets universally used the figure of the vine in describing Israel's unfaithfulness to God and His judgement against them (Hos. 10:1, Isa. 5:1-2, Ezek. 15:6). For instance, in Jer. 2:21, God says *"Yet I planted you a choice vine, a completely faithful seed. How then have you turned yourself before Me into the degenerate shoots of a foreign vine?"*

In the New Testament, Jesus adopts the Old Testament illustration of the vine, but applies it in describing Himself. It now denotes the Son of God instead of the people of God.

In John 15:1, Jesus states *"I am the true vine..."* The implication is that unlike unfaithful Israel, Jesus is faithful and true. He has satisfied all of the requirements that God expected of His people. Christ did what God's people could not. Because of His faithfulness, Jesus is the *"true vine"*.

Christ, the *"true vine"*, continuously imparts life to His spiritual branches, the church. The branch is not something outside of the vine, but is rather part of and dependent on the vine.

> *I am the vine, you are the branches; he who abides in Me and I in him, he bears much fruit, for apart from Me you can do nothing.*
> **–John 15:5**

A mother can only nurse an infant for a short period. The mother is not rich enough in life to continuously feed her growing offspring. This is not so with the vine. The vine is constantly feeding its branches. The branch cannot survive apart from the vine.

In our union with Christ, we find a new likeness to His nature. Rom. 6:5 says *"For if we have become united with Him in the likeness of His death, certainly we shall also be in the likeness of His resurrection."* Here, *"united"* is best translated as "grown together". We are grafted into Christ.

In Rom. 11:24, Paul illustrates this by saying that we were *"...by nature a wild olive tree, and were grafted contrary to nature into a cultivated olive tree...."* The wild olive is typical of our depraved nature. When it is grafted onto a good olive tree, there is enough force in the good olive tree to change the very nature of the wild olive branch.

This change in our nature leads to producing good fruit. In John 15:4, Jesus says *"Abide in Me, and I in you. As the branch cannot bear fruit of itself unless it abides in the vine, so neither can you unless you abide in Me."* Are you fruitful?

> *Bible verses for devotion:*
>
> **John 15:8**–How can we glorify God?
>
> **Col. 1:9-10**–How does fruit bearing both start with and lead to a growing personal knowledge of God?

Chapter 4

Union between Members and the Head of the Body

The figure of the members and Head of the Body illustrates our necessary link to Christ who directs, animates, and nurtures the church.

- Christ directs and orders the church.
- Christ expresses Himself through the church.
- Christ nourishes and nurtures the church.

All the members of the human body are united to their head which is the source of their activity and the power that controls their movements.

Likewise, all believers are members of an invisible body, the church, whose head is Christ. 1 Cor. 12:27 says *"Now you are Christ's body, and individually members of it."*

The church is all the persons whom Christ has saved, in whom He dwells, and to whom and through whom He reveals God. The church is nothing less than the body of Christ. As the head of the body directs the movement of its many members, so Christ directs His church.

Christ works in and through the church to accomplish His perfect will. In His wisdom, He has gifted and positioned each member of His body to bring glory to God. 1 Cor. 12:18 says *"But now God has placed the members, each one of them, in the body, just as He desired."*

Every single member of the church has a divinely appointed place and purpose in Christ because God has placed *"each one... just as He desired"*.

The church is a supernatural body manifesting the very glory of God. Through the church, God shows the fullness of His power and grace. In Christ, God loves us by imparting Himself to us. He fills and blesses us

> *And He put all things in subjection under His feet, and gave Him as head over all things to the church, which is His body, the fullness of Him who fills all in all.*
> **–Ephesians 1:22-23**

with "...*the fullness of Him who fills all in all*" (Eph. 1:23).

As Christ is the image of the invisible God, so too the church is appointed to be the image of the invisible Christ. Just as God can be seen only through Christ, so the Spirit of Christ can be seen only through the church.

Christ is "...*head over all things...*" for the benefit of the church (Eph. 1:22). Because the church is His body, Christ ensures that the church grows and flourishes. Ephesians 5:28-30 says "...*He who loves his own wife loves himself; for no one ever hated his own flesh, but nourishes and cherishes it, just as Christ also does the church, because we are members of His body.*"

Because the church is His body, Christ ensures its health as it grows both inwardly and outwardly. The church will "...*grow up in all aspects into Him who is the head, even Christ, from whom the whole body...causes the growth of the body for the building up of itself in love*" (Eph. 4:15-16).

Bible verses for devotion:

Colossians 1:18 –What does it mean for Christ to have supremacy? How is Christ supreme in the church?

Colossians 2:19– From Whom does the church grow? Who ensures the growth of the church?

Chapter 5

Union of Humanity with its beginning in Adam

The figure of humanity with its beginning in Adam illustrates how Christ is the source of new life and redemption for all believers.

- Christ is the second Man, the last Adam.
- Christ is the source of new life for every believer.
- Christ is the source of righteousness for every believer.

Scripture describes the whole human race as being one with the first man, Adam, through creation. In Adam, all of humanity fell from its relationship with God and derived a corrupted and guilty nature.

Scripture uses the figure of humanity with its beginning in Adam to help describe the new creation accomplished by Christ's redeeming love. The whole race of believers constitutes a new and restored humanity, whose purified and justified nature is derived from Christ, the second Man.

Christ is the source of new life for every believer. 1 Corinthians 15:21-22 says *"For since by a man came death, by a man also came the resurrection of the dead. For as in Adam all die, so also in Christ all will be made alive."*

The new life that comes through Christ is not just the lifting of sin's curse, but it is a new birth and transformation of the soul. In 1 Cor. 15:45, Paul teaches *"So also it is written, "The first man, Adam, became a living soul." The last Adam became a life-giving spirit."* The life that only Christ can impart is indeed life in abundance (John 10:10).

In the creation account, we find that Adam is first created and then woman is "...*taken out of Man*" (Gen 2:23). So, it is similarly with Christ and the church. We are members of Christ's body, because in Christ we have the principle of our

> *For as through the one man's disobedience the many were made sinners, even so through the obedience of the One the many will be made righteous.*
> –**Romans 5:19**

origin. From Christ our life arose, just as the life of Eve was derived from Adam.

The church is Christ's helpmate, formed out of Christ in His deep sleep of death, as Eve out of Adam. The church will therefore always be nearest to Christ, as Eve was to Adam.

Because Christ is the source of all spiritual life for His people, He is called, in Isaiah 9:6, "*Eternal Father*," and it is said, in Isaiah 53:10, that "...*He will see His offspring....*"

In Christ, the last Adam, we find the source of our righteousness. Because of Christ's perfectly obedient life, "...*many will be made righteous*" (Romans 5:19).

Rom. 5:12, 21 states "*Therefore, just as through one man sin entered into the world, and death through sin, and so death spread to all men, because all sinned— ... so that, as sin reigned in death, even so grace would reign through righteousness to eternal life through Jesus Christ our Lord.*"

Because Christ is the source of our righteousness and our new life, we are redeemed for holiness and eternal life (Rom. 6:22). God has certainly promised the church that "*Just as we have borne the image of the earthly, we will also bear the image of the heavenly*" (1 Corinthians 15:49).

Bible verse for devotion:

John 6:53– Do you have life apart from Christ?

II. DIRECT SCRIPTURAL
STATEMENTS OF THIS UNION

Chapter 6

The believer is said to be in Christ

The believer is said to be "in Christ" as the element or atmosphere, which surrounds him with its perpetual presence and which constitutes his vital breath.

- "In Christ" always means "in union with Christ"
- This phrase is the very key to the whole New Testament.
- "In Christ" points us to the Savior and His work for us.

Scripture asserts in the most direct and straightforward language the fact of our union with Christ through faith.

Lest we should regard the previously studied figures from the prior chapters as merely descriptive metaphors without basis in fact, let us examine how union with Christ is taught plainly and repeatedly in the New Testament. To list and carefully study every direct assertion of the believer's union with Christ would more than fill the space of this book.

One of the most common ways that our union with Christ is explained in the New Testament is that the believer is said to be "in Christ".

This phrase, "in Christ", always means "in union with Christ," wherever it is found in the New Testament. The phrase, "in Christ", is the very key to understanding Paul's epistles and to the whole New Testament. It conveys that believers are in Christ's presence and receive His salvation.

Airplane passengers travel higher, farther and faster because they are in a plane. They are even said to fly. So too, believers are truly in Christ and thus share His life and glory.

The phrase, "in Christ", is chiefly used to picture the benefits that Christ imparts to all those united to Him. For example: "...*alive to God in Christ Jesus*"

> ***Therefore if anyone is in Christ, he is a new creature; the old things passed away; behold, new things have come.***
> **–2 Corinthians 5:17**

(Rom. 6:11); "*Therefore there is now no condemnation for those who are in Christ Jesus*" (Rom. 8:1); "*For as in Adam all die, so also in Christ all will be made alive*" (1 Cor. 15:22); "*Therefore if anyone is in Christ, he is a new creature...*" (2 Cor. 5:17); "*...for you are all one in Christ Jesus*" (Gal. 3:28); "*But now in Christ Jesus you who formerly were far off have been brought near by the blood of Christ*" (Eph. 2:13).

Sometimes the phrase, "in Christ", is substituted with "in Me" or "in Him". Nevertheless, the meaning is still the same. For example: "*...you in Me...*" (Jn. 14:20); "*Abide in Me...*" (John 15:4, 5, 6, 7); "*just as He chose us in Him before the foundation of the world...*" (Eph. 1:4); "*...so that I may gain Christ, and may be found in Him...*" (Phil. 3:8-9); "*...we abide in Him...*" (1 John 4:13).

That the believer is truly in Christ is what is truly being symbolized in baptism. Gal. 3:27 says "*For all of you who were baptized into Christ have clothed yourselves with Christ.*" We are fully immersed into Christ the Savior. We are forever surrounded by His presence through the Holy Spirit.

After witnessing Christ's first miracle, "*...His disciples believed in Him*" (John 2:11). A more accurate translation is: "His disciples believed *into* Him". Believers receive Christ through faith so as to totally submerge themselves into Him.

> **Bible verses for devotion:**
>
> **Gal. 3:25-27**– How are we incorporated into Christ?

Chapter 7

Christy is said to be in the believer

Christ is said to be "in you", and so to live His life within the believer. Every believer can point to this as the dominating fact of their experience.

- "Christ in you" always means "in union with Christ".
- Christ is in the heart of every believer.
- Christ lives His life within and through every believer.

Union with Christ is often taught by stating that Christ is "in you". In John 14:20, Jesus pledges Himself to us saying, "*...I in you*". This amazing promise is true for every believer.

In Galatians 2:20, Paul writes "*I have been crucified with Christ; and it is no longer I who live, but Christ lives in me....*" Christians acknowledge this as the prevailing reality of their lives. As a dying patient is saved by a transfusion of blood, a believer lives by receiving Christ. It is not so much that the believer lives, as it is Christ who lives in the believer.

The phrase, "in you", is central to understanding the apostle Paul's epistles. Paul desires every believer to know the certainty and depth of their union with Christ. Paul stirringly asks the church "*....do you not recognize this about yourselves, that Jesus Christ is in you...*" (2 Cor. 13:5)? With like passion, Paul falls to his knees in prayer pleading "*that Christ may dwell in your hearts through faith...*" (Eph. 3:17). Paul emphasizes this because it is only through Christ living in us that we can know and experience the perfect love of God and be filled with His fullness and share in His glory.

"Christ in you" is thus the most lofty and grand revelation of God to men. Col. 1:26-27 tells us that "...*the mystery which has been hidden from the past ages and generations, but has now been manifested to His saints, to whom God willed to make*

> *I have been crucified with Christ; and it is no longer I who live, but Christ lives in me; and the life which I now live in the flesh I live by faith in the Son of God, who loved me and gave Himself up for me.*
> **–Galataians 2:20**

known what is the riches of the glory of this mystery among the Gentiles, which is Christ in you, the hope of glory."

Sometimes the phrase, "in you", is substituted with others such as "in me", "in us", or "in him". Nevertheless, the meaning is still the same. For example: "...*to reveal His Son in me...*" (Gal. 1:16); "...*He abides in us...*" (1 John 3:24); "...*and I in him*" (John 6:56); "...*I will come in to him...*" (Rev. 3:20). The Lamb of God abides in us. How sublime!

That Christ is truly in the believer is what is truly being symbolized in the Lord's Supper. Scripture asks "*Is not the cup of blessing which we bless a sharing in the blood of Christ? Is not the bread which we break a sharing in the body of Christ?*" (1 Cor. 10:16). It symbolizes His life in ours.

"Christ in you" drives us to glorify God for His divine life is manifested through ours. 2 Cor. 4:6-7 says "*For God, who said, "Light shall shine out of darkness," is the One who has shone in our hearts to give the Light of the knowledge of the glory of God in the face of Christ. But we have this treasure in earthen vessels, so that the surpassing greatness of the power will be of God and not from ourselves.*"

Bible verse for devotion:

1 Cor. 11:26– How is Christ incorporated into us?

Chapter 8

The Father, Son and Spirit dwell in the believer

Jesus Christ is said to dwell inside every believer. This indwelling must also be true of the Father and the Holy Spirit. The Father and the Son dwell in the believer, for where the Son is, there always the Father must be also. This indwelling is by the Holy Spirit.

- The Father and the Son are in the heart of every believer.
- The Father and Son dwell in believers by the Holy Spirit.

Union with Christ is expressed by stating that the Father and Son dwell inside believers. In John 14:10, Jesus asks *"Do you not believe that I am in the Father, and the Father is in Me? The words that I say to you I do not speak on My own initiative, but the Father abiding in Me does His works."* Jesus emphasizes this again in John 14:11 saying *"Believe Me that I am in the Father and the Father is in Me..."*

Hunters once threw bolas, which were projectiles linked together by cords. When one projectile connected with its target, so did the others. In like manner, where the Son is, there the Father must necessarily be also. Jesus promises every believer that *"...my Father will love him, and we will come unto him, and make our abode with him"* (Jn. 14:23).

John instructs believers that *"We have seen and testify that the Father has sent the Son to be the Savior of the world. Whoever confesses that Jesus is the Son of God, God abides in him, and he in God* (1 John 4:14-15). How lofty it is that the Father dwells in us through Christ and we're in Him!

The profound promise that the Father and the Son make their home in every believer is heightened by the realization of God's

> *Jesus answered and said to him, "If anyone loves Me, he will keep My word; and My Father will love him, and We will come to him and make Our abode with him.*
> **—John 14:23**

infinite love for His people. The beloved apostle writes *"We have come to know and have believed the love which God has for us. God is love, and the one who abides in love abides in God, and God abides in him"* (1 John 4:16).

Romans 5:5 teaches us that *"...the love of God has been poured out within our hearts through the Holy Spirit who was given to us."* The indwelling of the Father and the Son in our hearts whereby we know God's love is by the Holy Spirit.

Jesus promised His disciples *"I will ask the Father, and He will give you another Helper, that He may be with you forever; that is the Spirit of truth, whom the world cannot receive, because it does not see Him or know Him, but you know Him because He abides with you and will be in you"* (John 14:16-17). The Spirit was given to abide in us forever.

Jesus lovingly assured them that *"I will not leave you as orphans; I will come to you. After a little while the world will no longer see Me, but you will see Me; because I live, you will live also. In that day you will know that I am in My Father, and you in Me, and I in you"* (John 14:18-20).

Through the sending of the Holy Spirit, the Father and the Son are inseparably present in every believer at all times.

Bible verses for devotion:

1 John 3:23-24—How does the Father abide in us? How do we know that the Father abides in us? Who is it that is given to us?

Chapter 9

The believer has life by partaking of Christ

Scripture asserts that our union with Christ means that we have a participation or sharing in His very life. The believer has eternal life by partaking of Christ as Christ has life by partaking of the Father.

- We live by partaking of and thus participating in Christ.
- This participation is an actual sharing in Christ's life.
- Jesus likened this to Himself having life by the Father.

Jesus taught that believers can only have spiritual life through a participation in and partaking of His own life.

Jesus taught in John 6:33-35 *""For the bread of God is that which comes down out of heaven, and gives life to the world." Then they said to Him, "Lord, always give us this bread." Jesus said to them, "I am the bread of life; he who comes to Me will not hunger, and he who believes in Me will never thirst.""* Here, Jesus claims to be the giver and source of spiritual life. Just as our bodies need food and drink to live, we need Christ to live spiritually. His life sustains ours.

Christ's claim as the source and giver of spiritual life is exclusive. John 6:53 says *"So Jesus said to them, "Truly, truly, I say to you, unless you eat the flesh of the Son of Man and drink His blood, you have no life in yourselves.""*

Apart from Christ, we only know death. Jesus said *"This is the bread which came down out of heaven; not as the fathers ate and died; he who eats this bread will live forever"* (John 6:58). Partakers of Christ have eternal life.

To partake of Christ is to participate or share in His life. 1 Corinthians 10:16 asks *"Is not the cup of blessing which we bless a sharing in the blood of Christ? Is not the bread which we break a sharing in the body of Christ?"*

> *I am the living bread that came down out of heaven; if anyone eats of this bread, he will live forever; and the bread also which I will give for the life of the world is My flesh.*
> **–John 6:51**

The Lord's Supper pictures in the language of symbol the soul's actual participation in the very life of Christ. The word translated here as *"a sharing"* means not merely association or fellowship, but describes a real and concrete participation.

When John saw the ascended Christ, he wrote *"When I saw Him, I fell at His feet like a dead man. And He placed His right hand on me, saying, "Do not be afraid; I am the first and the last, and the living One; and I was dead, and behold, I am alive forevermore, and I have the keys of death and of Hades"* (Rev. 1:17-18). This is He Whose life we share!

The believer has life by partaking of Christ in a way that may not inappropriately be compared with Christ's having life by partaking of the Father. Jesus says in John 6:57 *"As the living Father sent Me, and I live because of the Father, so he who eats Me, he also will live because of Me."*

Because they share the same essential, original and underived life, the life of the Father guarantees the life of the Son. In like manner, Jesus promises us that *"...because I live, you will live also"* (John 14:19). United to Christ, He imparts to us *"...the power of an indestructible life"* (Heb. 7:16).

Bible verses for devotion:

John 1:1-4 –Where do we find life and light?

Chapter 10

All believers are one in Christ

Scripture proclaims that all believers are one in Christ, as Christ Himself is one with the Father.

- All believers are united to one another in Christ.
- Jesus likened this unity to His union with the Father.
- United believers testify of God's glory, salvation and love.
- We are united with all believers on earth and in heaven.

When Jesus's crucifixion was near, He prayed for His disciples. Jesus prayed "*...Holy Father, keep them in Your name, the name which You have given Me, that they may be one even as We are*" (John 17:11).

God had given His own name to Christ to reveal to His people. Jesus is praying for His disciples to be kept true to His own perfect revelation of God so that they may experience a unity among themselves that reflects the blessed fellowship between the Persons of the Trinity.

Jesus then expands this prayer to cover all believers in all ages. He asks "*that they may all be one; even as You, Father, are in Me and I in You, that they also may be in Us, so that the world may believe that You sent Me*" (Jn. 17:21).

A caboose is united to the locomotive and the other cars. When Jesus prays "*...that they may be in Us...*", He tells us that we are not only individually united to Christ, but we are also collectively united to Him as His people. Union with Christ is thus the presupposition of the church. This makes the church His supernatural body manifesting His own glory.

Christ unites His people to Himself and also to each other so *"...that the world may believe..."* that Christ was sent to save man.

> *At that day you will know that I am in My Father, and you in Me, and I in you.*
> —John 14:20

Jesus continues praying in John 17:22-23, saying *"The glory which You have given Me I have given to them, that they may be one, just as We are one; I in them and You in Me, that they may be perfected in unity, so that the world may know that You sent Me, and loved them, even as You have loved Me."*

In these verses, Jesus tells us that He has united His people to manifest His glory. God's glory is the vast weight of all His attributes. Jesus prays for us to be *"...perfected in unity..."*, meaning that we would be completed into one body that perfectly reflects the character of Christ our living Head.

As Christ's own body, the church is united together to collectively reflect Christ's glory, be living proof of Christ's gracious redemption, and to know God's everlasting love.

Old Testament believers were perfected only in the body of Christ (Heb. 11:40). The Church is thus united with all of the redeemed, both on earth and in heaven (Heb. 12:23). As we live for Christ here, so also do those saints who live in His heavenly presence. Christ holds us all together in His life. At His return, we will not precede those who fell asleep, but our bodies will be raised together in His image (1 Thess. 4:15-18).

Let us labor for one another and future generations until *"...all attain to the unity of the faith, and of the knowledge of the Son of God, to a mature man, to the measure of the stature which belongs to the fullness of Christ"* (Eph. 4:13).

> *Bible verse for devotion:*
> **Galatians 3:28**– Who are believers united in?

Chapter 11

Believers are made partakers of the divine nature

Believers are said to be made partakers of God's holy nature through the promises of Christ for His glory.

- God calls us to know Him in His glory and excellence.
- We know and see the glory of God through Jesus Christ.
- We are united to Christ through faith in His promises.

In 2 Peter 1:3, Peter exalts Jesus Christ whose "... *divine power has granted to us everything pertaining to life and godliness, through the true knowledge of Him who called us by His own glory and excellence.*"

It is through union with Christ that "*divine power has granted to us everything pertaining to life and godliness*", for all these things are in Christ. The life of Christ our Lord lives in us and overflows with His abundance through our faith in Him. Therefore it is said that "*...all things belong to you...*" when "*...you belong to Christ...*" (1 Cor. 3:22-23).

When we trust in Christ, we possess all precious things in Him and desire to be like Him. Christ is our divine-human Savior who has expressly revealed God through His perfect humanity and "*...called us by His own glory and excellence.*"

Peter teaches that God's glorious attributes and works both reveal Him and call us to Him. God's glory is the great sum of all His attributes. God's excellence is the activity of His attributes. Because holiness is God's self-affirmation and self-willing, God's glory and excellence beckon us to know Christ and to reflect His infinite perfection and purity.

We know and see the glory of God through the Person and work of Christ. 2 Peter 1: 4 says *"For by these He has granted to us His precious and magnificent promises, so that by them you may become partakers of the divine nature, having escaped the corruption that is in the world by lust."*

> *For of His fullness we have all received, and grace upon grace.*
> **—John 1:16**

Through God's promises, we *"become partakers of the divine nature."* It is not that we become God, but rather we share in God's life through union with Christ, the God-man.

We become partakers of the divine nature through faith in Christ. All of God's promises are accomplished in Christ. Christ is both the revelation of God and realization of His promises. Christ is thus the divine "Yes" and "Amen" (2 Cor. 1:20). In Christ alone we know God's fullness (Col. 2:9-10).

United to Christ, we are like the light bulb that is turned on and becomes radiant. His life starts to shine through ours. In Christ, we *"...put on the new self who is being renewed to a true knowledge according to the image of the One who created him"* (Col. 3:10). In Christ, *"...we all, with unveiled face, beholding as in a mirror the glory of the Lord, are being transformed into the same image from glory to glory, just as from the Lord, the Spirit"* (2 Cor. 3:18).

We will assuredly be renewed in the likeness of God for we have been *"...predestined to become conformed to the image of His Son..."* (Rom. 8:29). But we must lay hold of His promises. *"Therefore, having these promises, beloved, let us cleanse ourselves from all defilement of flesh and spirit, perfecting holiness in the fear of God"* (2 Cor. 7:1).

Bible verse for devotion:

2 Peter 3:18 –Who are we to grow into? To what end?

Chapter 12

The believer is made one spirit with the Lord

Human nature is so interpenetrated and energized by the divine that the two move and act as one.

- Believers are joined entirely to Christ by the closest bond.
- Believers have the Spirit of Christ living within them.
- Christ communicates Himself to us by the Holy Spirit.

When we are united to Christ through faith, we are made one spirit with Christ. 1 Corinthians 6:17 says *"But the one who joins himself to the Lord is one spirit with Him."*

To be joined to Christ means to be glued together. It is to adhere or cleave to Christ by the closest bond imaginable.

Our union with Christ is constant, undivided, thorough and sacred. Although man can divide mountains and split atoms, nothing can separate us from Christ (Rom. 8:38-39).

Our union with Christ surpasses the proximity of even the union between a husband and wife. We are nearer to Him than anything else can ever be. This union is so close that Christ is said to be He *"...who is our life..."* (Col. 3:4).

Our union with Christ is so intimate that we are *"...one spirit with Him."* To be one spirit with Christ is to have His Spirit *"...in you, whom you have from God"* (1 Cor. 6:19).

Christ is therefore the ultimate end where God promised *"I will put My Spirit within you, and you will come to life..."* and *"My dwelling place also will be with them; and I will be their God, and they will be My people"* (Ezekiel 37:14, 27).

Christ communicates Himself to the human spirit by the Person of the Holy Spirit. By the Holy Spirit, believers are brought into a common life with Christ. The Holy Spirit is *"...poured out upon us richly through Jesus Christ our Savior"* (Ti. 3:6).

> *There is one body and one Spirit, just as also you were called in one hope of your calling; one Lord, one faith, one baptism, one God and Father of all who is over all and through all and in all.*
> **–Ephesians 4:4-6**

Just as the Holy Spirit is given without measure to Christ (John 3:34), in like manner believers receive the abundance of Christ through the Holy Spirit. Just as Christ offered Himself without blemish unto God through the Holy Spirit (Heb. 9:14), so too, it is only through the Holy Spirit that the redemptive work of Christ is applied to believers.

Jesus promised that He would send His Spirit who *"...will take of Mine and will disclose it to you. All things that the Father has are Mine; therefore I said that He takes of Mine and will disclose it to you"* (John 16:14-15).

Christ has given us His Spirit as the spirit of regeneration (Jn. 3:3-8), of sanctification (Rom. 8:13), and as the seal and guarantee of our future glory (Eph. 1:14). He is the Advocate in our heart (Rom. 8:16) who is forever with us (Jn. 14:16).

The Spirit of Christ is so near to us, and so one with us that our prayer is called His, or rather, His prayer becomes ours (Romans 8:26). This impartation of Christ to the believer through His Spirit is so unreserved and complete that Romans 8:9 says *"... But if anyone does not have the Spirit of Christ, he does not belong to Him."*

Bible verses for devotion:

2 Cor. 3:17-18 –Do you behold Christ's glory? How?

III. WHAT THE NATURE OF THIS UNION IS NOT

Chapter 13

Union with Christ is not in parity of Constitution

Christ created all things in Himself and holds all things together in Himself for His own glory. This union of constitution prepares the way for that spiritual union where Christ joins Himself to us through faith.

- All things came into being through Christ.
- All things are held together in Christ.
- Christ created us and sustains us for His glory.

Every atom in the universe is the expression of the mind and will of Christ. Colossians 1:16 teaches us that *"For by Him all things were created, both in the heavens and on earth, visible and invisible, whether thrones or dominions or rulers or authorities—all things have been created through Him and for Him."*

Christ is the fount of all being. John 1:3-4 declares that *"All things came into being through Him, and apart from Him nothing came into being that has come into being. In Him was life, and the life was the Light of men."*

Here, Christ is said to be more than just the architect of the cosmos. Christ is said to be the very life of all things for life is *"In Him..."* (John 1:4). From center to circumference, all of life is in Christ. We affirm Paul's profound testimony *"For in Him we live and move and exist..."* (Acts 17:28).

Scripture contrasts the false gods and idols of this world with the one true Lord, *"... Jesus Christ, by whom are all things, and we exist through Him"* (1 Corinthians 8:6).

Hebrews 1:3 says Christ *"...upholds all things by the word of His power...."* The same voice that exclaimed *"It is finished!"* (John 19:30) at Golgotha is the same voice that illuminates the stars, sets boundaries to the seas, and sustains all life through and for Him.

Christ is the very glue which keeps the universe and all that it contains from chaos, disintegration and annihilation.

> *For by Him all things were created, both in the heavens and on earth, visible and invisible, whether thrones or dominions or rulers or authorities—all things have been created through Him and for Him. He is before all things, and in Him all things hold together.*
> **– Colossians 1:16-17**

Colossians 1:17 exalts Christs for *"He is before all things, and in Him all things hold together."* Every breath we take is by use of powers with which He has given us, and which He personally sustains. Every heart-beat is a testimony to His personal presence and activity within our physical frame.

But Christ also surpasses our constitution. He is not only immanent, but He is also transcendent. Christ is not only *"in all"* and *"through all"*, but also *"above all"* (Eph. 4:6).

Acts 17:24-27 says *"The God who made the world and all things in it...gives to all people life and breath and all things...that they would seek God, if perhaps they might grope for Him and find Him, though He is not far from each one of us."* God reveals Himself and calls us to Himself in Jesus Christ so that we may find Him. When we trust Christ, we find the holy relationship for which we were created.

Bible verses for devotion:

Colossians 2:10– How are we completed?

Chapter 14

Union with Christ is not in parity of Personality

Humanity was created by Christ in His image with a personal nature. This natural likeness prepares the way for that spiritual union where Christ joins Himself to us through faith for His glory.

- God created man to reflect His nature or personality.
- Even after his fall, man's natural likeness to God endures.
- Union with Christ doesn't destroy man's personal nature.

God is a personal being. This means God reflects, wills and acts from within by virtue of His own free will. God told Moses to tell Israel that *"I AM has sent me to you"* (Ex. 3:14). God is not the "IT IS" or "I WAS", but is the great everlasting "I AM". "I AM" implies both personality and presence.

Because God is a Person, He is relational. This means that God relates in His Tri-unity and also to His creation. At the root of His personality is infinite capacity for perfect love.

Genesis 1:27 says God created man *"in His own image"*. God created man in His likeness to be a personal being, both self-conscious and self-determining. By virtue of this personality, man could at his creation choose which of the objects of his knowledge (self, the world, or God) should be the norm and center of his affection and development.

Adam rejected God's authority and humanity fell away from God. However, man's natural likeness to God remains and is inalienable. It constitutes a capacity for redemption that gives value to all men (Gen. 9:6; Jam. 3:9; 1 Pet. 2:17).

Indeed, it constitutes the reason why Christ should die. Man was worth redeeming. The lost sheep, the lost piece of money, and the lost son were worth the effort to seek and save (Luke 15). Christ's death for man revealed the infinite worth of the human soul, and taught us to count all men as brethren for who we would die (Rom. 9:3).

> *"You are My witnesses," declares the LORD, "And My servant whom I have chosen, so that you may know and believe Me and understand that I am He. Before Me there was no God formed, and there will be none after Me. I, even I, am the LORD, and there is no savior besides Me."*
> *–Isaiah 43:10-11*

Jesus Christ came to save His people by uniting them to Himself. This union is not accomplished by having our own personal essence transferred or assumed into the essence of Christ. This would obliterate the personality and activity of the believer. We are redeemed in Christ, but not absorbed.

Likewise, it is impossible for Christ's pure and perfect nature to be changed, improved or diminished. Even in heaven, His infinite nature will always be distinct from ours.

We are indeed persons, but not fully our own masters. Our personality is incomplete. Our self-determination is as limited as our self-consciousness. We reason truly, only with God's helping. We will rightly, only as God works in us to will and to do His good pleasure (Phil. 2:13). Our love only abides in His higher love (1 Jn. 4:16). To make us truly ourselves, to be complete, we need an infinite Personality to supplement and energize our own. We find this only in union with Christ.

Bible verses for devotion:

Heb. 8:10-12– For what reason are we redeemed?

Chapter 15

Union with Christ is not in parity of Moral likeness

Humanity was created by Christ in His image with a holy nature. This original moral likeness is required for fellowship with God. This holy nature is restored only when Christ joins Himself to us through faith.

- Humanity was created in God's image to be holy.
- Humanity fell and our nature became corrupted by sin.
- This lost moral likeness can only be restored in Christ.

Genesis 1:26-27 records *"Then God said, "Let Us make man in Our image, according to Our likeness; and let them rule over the fish of the sea and over the birds of the sky and over the cattle and over all the earth, and over every creeping thing that creeps on the earth." God created man in His own image, in the image of God He created him; male and female He created them."*

One aspect of being created in God's image is having a personal likeness with God. To have a personal relationship with God also requires a moral likeness. This moral likeness or holy nature is necessary to being created in God's image.

Holiness is the fundamental attribute in God. Holiness is God's declaration and willing of His own infinite moral perfection and purity. Throughout Scripture, God constantly asserts His holiness. Even in heaven, where there is no sin, there is the same reiteration: *"Holy, holy, holy is the LORD of hosts"* (Isa. 6:3); *"Holy, holy, holy is the LORD God, the Almighty"* (Rev. 4:8). This is the momentum of God's being.

Since holiness is the fundamental attribute of God, this must also of necessity be the chief attribute of those created to be in His image

> *Behold, I have found only this, that God made men upright, but they have sought out many devices.*
> —Ecclesiastes 7:29

(Eph. 4:24; Col. 3:8-10). God created man with a direction of the affections and the will to reflect His moral likeness.

Newly created man had right moral tendencies, as well as freedom from actual fault. Otherwise the communion with God described in Genesis would not have been possible.

Though the first man was fundamentally good, he still had the power of choosing evil. There was a bent of the affections and will toward God, but man was not confirmed in holiness. Man's heart turned from God and was corrupted.

The loss of this moral likeness to God was the chief calamity of the Fall. Man has defaced the image of God in his moral corruption, even though the image of God in its personal or natural aspect is enduring. As Pascal said, man is now both "the glory and the scandal of the universe."

Man is like a shattered mirror. We can't restore our lost likeness (Rom. 3:20). Ps. 5:4 says *"For You are not a God who takes pleasure in wickedness; No evil dwells with You."*

Yet Christ unites Himself to us and freely gives *"even the righteousness of God through faith in Jesus Christ for all those who believe...* (Rom. 3:22). We are restored in Christ.

The dignity of human nature consists not so much in what man is, but in what God meant him to be, and in what he will become when the lost image of God is fully restored.

Bible verses for devotion:

   Rom. 3:20-28– Why can't moral attainment save us?

Chapter 16

Union with Christ is not in parity with Faith

Faith saves only in connection with the Savior. Faith receives Christ in our regeneration by the Holy Spirit.

- Faith apart from union with the Savior is impotent.
- Faith is only saving when its object is Christ the Savior.
- Faith receives Christ and His saving work as our own.

Faith is indeed the means of salvation. Scripture declares *"For by grace you have been saved through faith; and that not of yourselves, it is the gift of God"* (Eph. 2:8). Note that we are not saved by faith, or on account of faith, but only *"through"* faith. Faith is not the means of salvation because it has any value in and of itself. Faith is the means of salvation only as it receives Christ the Savior. The Holy Spirit opens our heart and we receive Christ (Acts 16:14).

Faith is not an intellectual notion that there is a Christ. Faith is rational, but it is not simply an idea of the intellect.

Faith is not a stirring of the feelings concerning Christ. Faith is affecting, but it is not simply an emotional response.

Faith is primarily an act of the will. It is the act of the will that surrenders to Christ as Lord and receives Him as Savior. Saving faith is responding and receiving, consecration and appropriation, giving and taking (Matthew 11:28-30).

Therefore faith is not merely intellectual or affecting, but is volitional. Faith is a person, a sinner, committing himself to another person, a Savior. It is the response of our renewed will in giving ourselves to Christ and receiving Him as Savior.

Through faith we "*...have received Christ Jesus the Lord...*" and "*...walk in Him*" (Col. 2:6).

Paul commends the Corinthian church for their receptivity of the good news of Jesus Christ

> *And there is salvation in no one else; for there is no other name under heaven that has been given among men by which we must be saved.* —Acts 4:12

"*...which also you received, in which also you stand*" (1 Cor. 15:1). To receive Christ, to walk in Him and to stand in Him implies a sense of realization, a making the matter a reality.

When we receive a gift, we don't receive a reflection or a shadow. We receive that which is substantial and real. So it is with faith. We receive Christ as real, living and present in us.

When we receive a gift, it becomes our own. So it is with faith. Faith appropriates Christ. To receive Christ is to have and possess Him as our Lord and Savior. It is to joyfully say "*My beloved is mine, and I am his...*" (Song. 2:16).

Faith counts all that Christ is and does as our own. Faith connects the objective person and external work of Christ to us. To receive Christ is to take Him as the revelation of God, lay claim to Him as ours, and participate in His resurrection.

The hope of faith is not in the facts that we believe, but in Christ whom we receive. The glory of faith is not in how we are affected, but in the Savior to whom we are connected. The gospel is "*...Believe in the Lord Jesus, and you will be saved...*" (Acts 16:31). Too often we confuse salvation with the experience of our faith. We question if our finite intellect fully understood or if our fleeting feelings fully engaged, but these don't save. Let Christ our Savior be our hope and glory.

Bible verse for devotion:

Romans 6:23–Who is the free gift of God?

Chapter 17

Union with Christ is not in parity with Association

We form personal associations based on love or on a common purpose. Union with Christ is different in that it is an interpenetration of our person with His Person.

- We associate with others in mutual friendship and love.
- We associate with others in a mutual purpose.
- Union with Christ isn't external. It is radically pervasive.

Scripture speaks of personal associations based on the deep fellowship of friendship and love. The Old Testament says "...*the soul of Jonathan was knit with the soul of David, and Jonathan loved him as his own soul*" (1 Samuel 18:1). Likewise, the New Testament says that the early believers are said to have been "...*of one heart and one soul...*" (Acts 4:32).

Scripture speaks of personal associations based on common purposes or goals. The Old Testament says that those who rebuilt Jerusalem's wall labored with a singular prurpose of heart (Neh. 4:6). The New Testament says Paul found Aquilla and Priscilla in Corinth "*and because he was of the same trade, he stayed with them and they were working, for by trade they were tent-makers*" (Acts 18:3).

Apart from Christ, these bonds of love and purpose are external to us and temporal in nature. They have an ebb and flow. Friendships can grow, wane or end. Objectives may be fufilled, neglected, or abandoned. We can chose to associate or dissassociate based on our circumstance and desires. Only in Christ can these bonds prove to be enduring and fulfilling.

Christ's union with His people is distinguished from any mere external association. Jesus prayed for His people *"that they may all be one; even as You, Father, are in Me and I in You, that they also may be in Us..."* (Jn. 17:21).

In this prayer, Jesus asked that believers would be united together as one just as the Father and Son are united together as One.

> *Now on the last day, the great day of the feast, Jesus stood and cried out, saying, "If anyone is thirsty, let him come to Me and drink. He who believes in Me, as the Scripture said, 'From his innermost being will flow rivers of living water.'"*
> **–John 7:37-38**

Even more incredibly, Jesus asks that all believers would be united into the life of the Triune God. In God's Tri-Unity there is perfect communion for there alone divine affection meets its perfect object. There is no more perfect intimacy and self-impartation than the perfect knowledge and love that is between the Persons of the Triune God (Jn. 17:25-26).

We are brought into this perfect communion through Christ who indwells us (Eph. 3:14-17). When Christ pervades our person with His Person, we are made perfect in His body and perfectly loved for His sake (Jn. 17:23). Christ permeates our *"...innermost being..."* and His life flows out (John 7:38).

Union with Christ isn't local church membership, church attendance, or embracing the title of Christian. Union with Christ isn't prayer, Bible study or discipleship. It isn't enough for us to be merely in touch with Christ. Christ, who is the root of David must become our root as well (Rev. 22:16-17).

Bible verse for devotion:

Jn. 6:56–Consider how close our union is with Him!

Chapter 18

Union with Christ is not in parity with Sentiment

Our feelings and thoughts about Christ do not unite us to Him. Union with Christ is not a mere contemplation. Union with Christ is union with an everlasting Savior.

- Union with Christ is not a feeling or an emotional state.
- Union with Christ is not an intellectual conception.
- Union with Christ brings life by His Word and Spirit.

Just as we are not united to Christ by external bonds of association, neither are we united to Christ by our internal sentiments regarding Him. A subjective union grounded in the feelings and thoughts of an individual is not a true and enduring bond at all.

Our union with Christ is not equal to our ever changing feelings and passions. We are fickle in our feelings and emotions. What we certainly love at one moment, we can greatly hate the very next moment (2 Sam. 13:5).

In Jer. 17:9, God said *"The heart is more deceitful than all else and is desperately sick; Who can understand it?"*

If our union with Christ was based in our emotional sentiments, we would have no union at all. We would be like *"Those on the rocky soil...who, when they hear, receive the word with joy; and these have no firm root; they believe for a while, and in time of temptation fall away"* (Luke 8:13).

Likewise, our union with Christ is not equal to our thoughts or contemplations of Him. Our attention to rational endeavors are just as fickle as our feelings and passions.

God is infinite, but man is finite. Our attention and intellect are limited.

Job 11:7 asks *"Can you discover the depths of God? Can you discover the limits of the Almighty?"*

If our union with Christ was based in our thoughts and ideas of Him, we would have no union at all. As love of God is a condition of

> *For My thoughts are not your thoughts, nor are your ways My ways, declares the LORD. For as the heavens are higher than the earth, so are My ways higher than your ways, and My thoughts than your thoughts.*
> –Isaiah 55:8-9

divine knowledge, our sin and love of self would keep us from union with Him. It would be said of us *"For even though they knew God, they did not honor Him as God or give thanks, but they became futile in their speculations, and their foolish heart was darkened"* (Rom. 1:21).

Union with Christ can never be mere sentiment. If it was, then we would hopelessly be like *"...clouds without water, carried along by winds; autumn trees without fruit, doubly dead, uprooted; wild waves of the sea, casting up their own shame like foam; wandering stars, for whom the black darkness has been reserved forever..."* (Jude 12-13).

In union with Christ, a new heart is created full of all Godly passions and holy emotions (Col. 3:12-15). In union with Christ, a new mind is given that is filled with the word of Christ and thus all wisdom and devotion (Col. 3:16-17).

We are united to Christ through faith by His Spirit. By the Word and Spirit, we are inseparably grounded in His life.

Bible verse for devotion:

John 6:63–What does the Word and Spirit give?

Chapter 19

Union with Christ is not in parity with Ordinances

Union with Christ is not mediated or conditioned by observances of Baptism and the Lord's Supper.

- Baptism and the Lord's Supper are ordained by Christ.
- Ordinances do not confer, modify or maintain our union.
- They externally picture our preceding union with Christ.

Baptism was instituted by Christ and practiced by the apostles (Matt. 28:19). Baptism is symbolic of a believer's union with Christ in which they are redeemed (Rom. 6:3-6). It externally pictures the reality of the believer's life in Christ.

Baptism is token of union with Christ in His death and resurrection where we are freed from sin's tyranny. Baptism doesn't confer, alter or enhance our union with Christ, but treasures and heralds it (Acts 10:47). As it pictures our union with Christ, we must never baptize unbelievers (Gal. 3:27).

The Lord's Supper was instituted by Christ and practiced by the apostles (Luke 22:19-20). The Supper symbolizes our union with Christ in His death and resurrection by which we are sustained and perfected (Matt. 26:26-29; Rev. 19:7-9). It externally pictures the reality of Christ's life in the believer.

The Lord's Supper is token of union with Christ in His death and resurrection by which we live. It speaks of joy and constant dependence on Christ for life. The Supper doesn't join us to Christ or modify our union, but indeed celebrates it and reveres the Savior (Acts 2:41-43, 46). As it pictures our union with Christ, it is never for unbelievers (1 Cor. 10:16).

Faith receives what is purely invisible and supersensible. Only faith receives and retains Christ the Redeemer, not the act of the body submitting to Baptism or partaking of the Supper.

> *Go therefore and make disciples of all the nations, baptizing them in the name of the Father and the Son and the Holy Spirit, teaching them to observe all that I commanded you; and lo, I am with you always, even to the end of the age.*
> *–Matthew 28:19-20*

The Ordinances will not render the presence of Christ to us in any way different than how Christ already has been united to us prior to our observing them.

Christ does not give us more of Himself when we get wet. Christ is not more real or more present when we eat. Where does a vine end and its branch begin? Can a building belong more to its foundation? Can a head be tied closer to its body?

To deny this is to fundamentally misunderstand both the certitude and the very nature of our union with Christ. To deny this is to come perilously close to speaking like Thomas and acting like the Galatians (John 20:25; Galatians 3:1-3). To deny this is to join those who seek a greater dispensation of the Spirit of Christ under the shadow of a sign than the full measure received in regeneration by the Spirit's brooding.

We must never confuse our already established union with Christ with the divine fellowship that results from it. Through the ordinary means of grace, our love for Christ and our knowledge of Christ will only increase and forever grow, but our union with Him will never be nearer or more real. Christ is truly and fully in us now and we are surely in Him.

> *Bible verses for devotion:*
> **Acts 2:36-42**–Who is received before the Ordinances?

IV. WHAT THE NATURE OF THIS UNION IS

Chapter 20

Union with Christ is an Organic Union

In Union with Christ we are partakers of His Person, members of His body and recipients of His love.

- We are connected to the whole of Christ.
- All who are in Him are connected members of His body.
- We live and long for Him and He lives and longs for us.

John's Gospel declares *"In the beginning was the Word, and the Word was with God, and the Word was God....And the Word became flesh, and dwelt among us, and we saw His glory, glory as of the only begotten from the Father, full of grace and truth"* (John 1:1; 14).

In the Incarnation, human and divine nature are united in Jesus Christ to reconcile God to man and man to God. The precise way in which the human and divine natures are united in the Person of Christ is unrevealed to us. But we can describe the two natures as perfect, distinct and inseparable.

Because Christ took on human nature, we can be united to Him in His humanity. Yet we are thereby united to His whole Person. In Scripture's testimony of Christ, there is never any separation of the human from the divine, or of the divine from the human. All that Jesus Christ spoke, did and accomplished for us was by the one Person, the God-man.

Scripture testifies that all who are united to Christ are connected members of His body. As members of His body, we are connected to each other as fellow believers and we are connected to Christ Himself who is our Husband and Head.

When we say something is organic, we mean that it is characterized as one whole composed of individual parts that function reciprocally.

> *So husbands ought also to love their own wives as their own bodies. He who loves his own wife loves himself; for no one ever hated his own flesh, but nourishes and cherishes it, just as Christ also does the church, because we are members of His body.*
> **–Ephesians 5:28-30**

For example, the body is an organism. In a body, limbs exist for the heart and heart for the limbs, and limbs and heart for the whole body.

Romans 12:4-5 says *"For just as we have many members in one body and all the members do not have the same function, so we, who are many, are one body in Christ, and individually members one of another."* This means that the church is united together and living for each other since we are Christ's body and we are living for Him.

Each member of His body lives and longs for Christ, our Husband and Head. Our heartbeat is that Christ may *"...be exalted in my body, whether by life or by death"* (Phil. 1:20).

Reciprocally, Christ lives for His members. Our Husband and Head loves His bride as His own body. Paul writes that Christ *"...is the head of the church, He Himself being the Savior of the body..."* Who *"...loved the church and gave Himself up for her, so that He might sanctify her, having cleansed her by the washing of water with the word, that He might present to Himself the church in all her glory, having no spot or wrinkle or any such thing; but that she would be holy and blameless"* (Ephesians 5:23-27).

Bible verses for devotion:

Hebrews 7:24-25–Who does Christ live for?

Chapter 21

Union with Christ is a Vital Union

Union with Christ is a vital union in which Christ's life becomes the dominating principle within us.

- A vital union that interpenetrates our person with His.
- A vital union where Christ is the very life of the believer.
- A vital union where Christ shares His fullness and glory.

The mystery of the gospel is "*...Christ in you, the hope of glory*" (Col. 1:27). The great news that Christ Jesus came into the world to save sinners is what we proclaim "*...so that we may present every man complete in Christ*" (Col. 1:28).

This revealed mystery declares that man does not have to be alienated from the life of God. By God's grace, man can be moved from being a mere tangent to the circle of the divine nature into the very life of God through union with Christ. In receiving Christ through faith, there is an interpenetration of our person with the Person of Christ by the Holy Spirit.

This vital union is distinct from any external association. Likewise, this vital interpenetration is far different from any sentimental notions of the heart or even theological musings in our minds. This vital union involves our entire being.

Christ interpenetrates our person with His Person. This means Christ lives in us and we live in Him. There is no part of us left untouched by Christ. The sap of the Vine runs into Its branches. This intertwining is absolutely necessary for believers to have new life. This union is as vital as having the same blood coursing through our veins (John 6:56-57).

As a result of this interpenetration, the living omnipresent Christ becomes the present spiritual life of every one united to Him (Colossians 3:4).

> *For you have died and your life is hidden with Christ in God. When Christ, who is our life, is revealed, then you also will be revealed with Him in glory.*
> **–Colossians 3:3-4**

We are not separate persons linked together by some temporary bond of friendship. Christ and the believer share the very same life.

Christ does not work upon us from without as if He was separated from us. Christ works in us from within. His heart is the heart from which the life-blood of our spirit flows.

When Paul states that "...*it is no longer I who live, but Christ lives in me...*" (Gal. 2:20), when he speaks of "...*Christ who is our life...*"(Col. 3:4), when he says, "*For to me, to live is Christ...*" (Phil. 1:21), Paul can only be understood as meaning that the life of Christ the risen Savior subjugates and permeates his whole life and defines his very existence.

Sharing in Christ's life is a sharing in His Sonship with the Father. All of the love, access, favor, joy, glory, exaltation, and inheritance that Christ has with the Father becomes ours. This amazing fullness of participation "*is with the Father, and with His Son Jesus Christ*" (1 John 1:3).

In the whole of His last discourse, Jesus taught us that mere external association or internal sentiment would not be sufficient for us. Jesus taught "...*apart from Me you can do nothing*" (Jn. 15:5). The heart of Christ's High Priestly Prayer is that we would be vitally joined to Himself for His glory.

Bible verses for devotion:

John 14:10, 23– Are these merely peripheral unions?

Chapter 22

Union with Christ is a Spiritual Union

> *Union with Christ is a spiritual union whose author and source is the Holy Spirit.*

- Union with Christ is a union of spirit not of body.
- Union with Christ is originated by the Holy Spirit.
- Union with Christ is maintained by the Holy Spirit.

Our union with Christ is a union of spirit. Union with Christ is not our physical constitution even though Christ in His immanence is everywhere within our physical frame.

When we are joined to Christ, we become one spirit with Him (1 Cor. 6:17). This means that His Spirit abides in us.

Although this is indeed a spiritual union, it unites us entirely to Christ. Man is represented in Scripture as having a two-fold nature of body and soul (or spirit), yet man is always related to as an organic unity, a whole man. It is man who transgresses and is accountable to God, not his soul or body independently. Therefore, Christ redeems us as a whole man, body and soul, for divine fellowship (Matt. 10:28-32).

In union with the Savior, we are so closely joined to Christ that our bodies belong to Him and are truly "...*the temple of the Holy Spirit who is in you*..." that we might be Christ's own members to "...*glorify God*..."(1 Cor. 6:19-20).

Union with Christ originates with the Holy Spirit. The Holy Spirit is the principle of all movement toward God. It is the Holy Spirit that quickens the sinner. Jesus said to enter His kingdom, you must be "...*born of the Spirit*" (Jn. 3:3-8).

The Holy Spirit is the Spirit of Christ. The Holy Spirit is sent by both the Father and the Son, to reveal Christ, apply His perfect work to our hearts, and render the Savior forever with us.

As the dispenser of divine grace, only the Holy Spirit can apply Christ's redeeming work to humantiy (1 Cor. 6:11).

> *In Him, you also, after listening to the message of truth, the gospel of your salvation—having also believed, you were sealed in Him with the Holy Spirit of promise, who is given as a pledge of our inheritance, with a view to the redemption of God's own possession, to the praise of His glory.*
> **–Ephesians 1:13-14**

The Spirit's work is in conviction and revelation (John 16:8). The Spirit's work is in quickening the sinner. Eze. 37:14 says *"I will put My Spirit within you, and you will come to life...."* As Christ is God's external revelation, His Spirit is His internal revelation. Only the Holy Spirit can give us an inward apprehension of Christ.

Through the working and indwelling of the Holy Spirit, God in His Person of Son was fully incarnate in Christ (Acts 10:38). Likewise, Christ is personally present in us and we are forever in Him through the Holy Spirit (John 14:16-20).

The Holy Spirit, who originates our union with Christ, must also maintain it. He does this from within us. He is not a visiting guest, but a resident. Paul asked the Father *"that He would grant you, according to the riches of His glory, to be strengthened with power through His Spirit in the inner man, so that Christ may dwell in your hearts through faith..."* and that we may forever exalt God (Eph. 3:16-17, 21).

Bible verses for devotion:

1 Cor. 12:12-13 –How are we united to Christ?

Chapter 23

Union with Christ is an Indissoluble Union

Union with Christ can never be dissolved.

- An indestructible union consistent with His Presence.
- An indestructible union consistent with His Power.
- An indestructible union consistent with His Promises.
- An indestructible union consistent with His Purposes.

Christ is our chief cornerstone who is tested, costly and firmly placed (Isa. 28:16). We belong to Christ being divinely fitted in permanent connection to Him (Eph. 2:20-22).

Believers are indissolubly joined to Christ as they share the very same life (Col 3:3-4). As the life of the Father guarantees the life of the Son, so Christ's indestructible life guarantees ours for He abides in us (Heb. 7:16; Jn. 6:57).

When we are joined to Christ, we become one spirit with Him (1 Cor. 6:17). When we place our faith in Christ, we are *"...sealed in Him with the Holy Spirit of promise"* (Eph. 1:13). This means that Christ is personally and inseparably present in us, and that we are and will forever be in Christ through the indwelling of the Holy Spirit (John 14:16-20).

Christ's omnipresence makes it possible for Him to be united to, and to be fully present in each believer as perfectly and truly as if that believer were the only one to receive Him.

Every believer has the whole Christ with him as his source of life, righteousness and every good thing. Every believer receives His infinite regard, affection and care. We may joyfully say that we have His undivided attention.

The omnipresence of Christ that renders Him fully present to care for every believer can't be separated from His omnipotence. Jesus said *"My sheep hear My voice, and I know them, and they follow Me; and I give eternal life to them, and they will never perish; and no one will snatch them*

> *For I am convinced that neither death, nor life, nor angels, nor principalities, nor things present, nor things to come, nor powers, nor height, nor depth, nor any other created thing, will be able to separate us from the love of God, which is in Christ Jesus our Lord.*
> –Romans 8:38-39

out of My hand. My Father, who has given them to Me, is greater than all; and no one is able to snatch them out of the Father's hand. I and the Father are one" (John 10:27-30).

Our union is sure because of His unchanging promises. At His ascension, Christ said *"...lo, I am with you always, even to the end of the age"* (Matt. 28:20). Christ's promises must always be certain for He is always true (1 John 5:20).

Our union is based in His eternal purposes (2 Tim. 1:9). We are chosen *"...in Him before the foundation of the world ...according to His purpose who works all things after the counsel of His will"* (Eph. 1:4, 11). His counsel will never fail.

Christ, as Head, will never cast off members of His body. Christ, as Husband, will never cast off His bride. Christ has *"...become one flesh"* with His church (Eph. 5:31-32).

"Jesus Christ is the same yesterday and today and forever" (Heb. 13:8). Our union is not maintained by us, but by His unchanging presence, power, promises and purposes.

Bible verses for devotion:

2 Cor. 1:21-22 –How are you established and sealed?

Chapter 24

Union with Christ is an Unfathomable Union

Union with Christ is unfathomable in its gracious love, unrivaled intimacy, transforming power and formation.

- Union with Christ is not unintelligible to the Christian.
- Union with Christ is not unexperienced by the Christian
- It is unfathomable in breadth, length, height and depth.

Our union is not unfathomable in being unintelligible to us or beyond the reach of our experience. We have ample Scriptural representations and direct statements that help us comprehend our union with Christ. Likewise, all believers know Christ and have access by His Spirit to the Father (Eph. 2:17-22). We know this because *"The Spirit Himself testifies with our spirit that we are children of God"* (Rom. 8:16).

We call it unfathomable because of the wideness of God's grace. Paul was awed by this when he wrote *"To me, the very least of all saints, this grace was given, to preach to the Gentiles the unfathomable riches of Christ"* (Eph. 3:8). By God's boundless love in Christ, we are reconciled, redeemed, set free, made alive, made just, blessed, commissioned, adopted, given a holy walk, and glorified. Along with David, we sing *"He brought me forth also into a broad place; He rescued me, because He delighted in me"* (Psalm 18:19).

We call it unfathomable because the intimacy of our union knows no equal. It surpasses any other union of souls that we know and so cannot be fully described or understood by earthly analogies. Our union with Christ is so far beyond our scope that we must pray to comprehend it (Eph. 3:19).

We call it unfathomable because of the transforming power of its influence. Our life is raised up into His own. While maintaining our own individuality, we are so interpenetrated and energized by the Spirit of Christ that it is impossible to pinpoint where our life ends and Christ's life begins. It seemed quite natural for

> *But let him who boasts boast of this, that he understands and knows Me, that I am the Lord who exercises lovingkindness, justice and righteousness on earth; for I delight in these things," declares the Lord.*
> –Jeremiah 9:24

Paul to write "...*work out your salvation with fear and trembling; for it is God who is at work in you, both to will and to work for His good pleasure*" (Phil. 2:12-13).

We call it unfathomable because the precise way in which we are joined to Christ by the Holy Spirit is a deep mystery to us. Jesus said "*The wind blows where it wishes and you hear the sound of it, but do not know where it comes from and where it is going; so is everyone who is born of the Spirit*" (John 3:8). We marvel at the Tri-Unity of God. We wonder at the miracle of the Incarnation. So too we will never fathom how we are individually joined to Christ with all the saints by His Spirit and made to be sons of God.

Upon our conversion, we may not grasp the nature of our union with Christ. We may think Christ to be only outside of us. Graciously, the apprehension of an external Savior is not separable from the reception of the internal Savior. Thus, the Way leads, through the Truth, to the Life (John 14:6). Christ is first the Door of the sheep, but in Him, after we have once entered in, we find abundant pasture (John 10:7-10).

Bible verses for devotion:

Rom. 11:33-36– Where does your wonder lead to?

V. CONSIDER YOUR UNION: HOPE AND GLORY FOR EVERY CHRISTIAN

Chapter 25

United to Christ by God's Gracious Purpose

We are chosen in Christ by God's grace alone to be His own people and to always live for His glory.

- We are chosen in Christ according to God's purposes.
- We are chosen in Christ despite our lack of merit.
- We are chosen in Christ so our glory will be in Him.

One of the great assurances that God has given to His people is that we are chosen by God to be in Christ by His Spirit through faith before time even began. This assures us that we are His own people, that we will always be in Christ, and that we will one day perfectly reflect the glory of Christ.

Scripture proclaims that "...*God has chosen you from the beginning for salvation through sanctification by the Spirit and faith in the truth. It was for this He called you through our gospel, that you may gain the glory of our Lord Jesus Christ*" (2 Thessalonians 2:13-14).

How comforting it is that we have been chosen by the Father for union with the Son by regeneration of His Spirit. Our union was foreordained in Christ before our creation so that we would share in the glory of Christ (Eph. 1:9-12).

We are chosen by God to be in Christ for there is no other Savior than Jesus Christ. Scripture says "...*He chose us in Him before the foundation of the world, that we would be holy and blameless before Him in love. He predestined us to adoption as sons through Jesus Christ to Himself, according to the kind intention of His will*" (Ephesians 1:4-5).

We are chosen *"according to the kind intention of His will"*. God chose us in Christ not because of our merit, but because of His special love for us. Moses teaches us *"The LORD did not set His love on you nor choose you because you were more in number than any of the peoples, for you were the fewest of all peoples, but because the LORD loved you..."* (Deut. 7:7-8).

> *But God has chosen the foolish things of the world to shame the wise, and God has chosen the weak things of the world to shame the things which are strong, and the base things of the world and the despised God has chosen, the things that are not, so that He may nullify the things that are, so that no man may boast before God.*
> **–1 Corinthians 1:27-29**

We are awestruck by God *"who has saved us and called us with a holy calling, not according to our works, but according to His own purpose and grace which was granted us in Christ Jesus from all eternity"* (2 Tim. 1:9).

God chose the foolish, weak, lowly, and despised—the nothings—when He chose us to be in Christ (1 Cor. 1:27-29).

We are chosen to be in Christ to glorify Him. Peter writes *"But you are A CHOSEN RACE, A royal PRIESTHOOD, A HOLY NATION, A PEOPLE FOR God's OWN POSSESSION, so that you may proclaim the excellencies of Him who has called you out of darkness into His marvelous light; for you once were NOT A PEOPLE, but now you are THE PEOPLE OF GOD; you had NOT RECEIVED MERCY, but now you have RECEIVED MERCY"* (2 Peter 2:9-10).

> **Bible verse for devotion:**
>
> **Eph. 1:4-6, 11-12**–His gracious choice results in what?

Chapter 26

United to Christ by God's Gracious Work

By God's gracious agency, we are made alive through our perfect union with Christ to be with Him forever.

- Our union with Christ is the work of God alone.
- Only God can make us new creatures in Christ Jesus.
- As union with Christ is God's work, it can't be undone.

God set His love on us in eternity past when the Father graciously chose us in Christ to be His own people. Not only did God choose us to be in union with Christ, but it is only by His agency that we are brought into our union with Christ.

Scripture give all the credit to God for the union of Christ with His church. Paul makes this very clear in teaching us *"...that no man may boast before God. But by His doing you are in Christ Jesus..."* (1 Corinthians 1:29-30).

Paul begins his first letter to Corinthian church by giving thanks for *"the grace of God which was given you in Christ Jesus"* (1 Cor. 1:4). Paul is giving gratitude here to God for their union with Christ. He gives thanks for every aspect of being in Christ including our conversion, growth, assurance, gifting, certain hope and sanctification. Paul exalts our God who *"...is faithful, through whom you were called into fellowship with His Son, Jesus Christ our Lord"* (1 Cor. 1:9).

In this passage, *"called"* means not merely to be pursued or invited, but conveys the effectual sense of being appointed or placed in Christ just as Paul himself was *"...called as an apostle of Jesus Christ by the will of God..."* (1 Cor. 1:1).

Paul had a vivid first hand understanding of God's agency in uniting us to Christ: his very own calling on the road to

> *But by His doing you are in Christ Jesus...*
> −1 Corinthians 1:30

Damascus. Paul thus wrote *"...if anyone is in Christ, he is a new creature; the old things passed away; behold, new things have come. Now all these things are from God, who reconciled us to Himself through Christ..."* (2 Cor. 5:17-18).

Paul gave all credit to God for anyone being in Christ, for regeneration only comes from God. May we say with Paul, *"But by the grace of God I am what I am..."* (1 Cor. 15:10).

John was likewise quick to give all the credit to God for joining us to Christ. John said we are in Christ through faith because we *"...were born, not of blood nor of the will of the flesh nor of the will of man, but of God"* (John 1:13).

While God turns men to Himself (Ps. 85:4; Song. 1:4; Jer. 31:18; Lam. 5:21), men are exhorted to turn themselves to God (Pr. 1:23; Isa. 31:6; 59:20; Eze. 14:6; 18:32; 33:9, 11; Joel 2:12-14). While God is represented as the author of the new heart and the new spirit (Ps. 51:10; Eze. 11:19; 36:26), men are commanded to make for themselves a new heart and spirit (Eze. 18:31; 2 Cor. 7:1; Phili. 2:12-13; Eph. 5:14).

This twofold depiction is only explained in that man is interpenetrated and quickened by God without destroying man's freedom, but in making him free in union with Christ.

When we repent and believe in Christ, we learn that God has gone before us to place us into union with Christ. As our union is authored by God, it is perfectly secured. Jesus said *"All that the Father gives Me will come to Me, and the one who comes to Me I will certainly not cast out"* (John 6:37).

Bible verses for devotion:

Matt. 11:25-30–Do we glorify God for His work?

Chapter 27

United to Christ who is God's Wisdom for us

We are united to Christ who is the reason, wisdom and power of God. All divine revelation, whether generally or specially revealed, is mediated by Christ.

- Christ is the only revealer of the Father.
- Apart from Christ, we would not know God's holiness.
- Apart from Christ, we would not know God's love.

Christ is not only called the Son of God, but is also called the Word of God. Scripture says *"In the beginning was the Word, and the Word was with God, and the Word was God. He was in the beginning with God"* (John 1:1-2).

As the Word of God, Christ is the only revelation of God to both Himself and to His creatures. Christ mediates the Father's thoughts, words and actions. From before creation, Christ existed as the expression of God to Himself. Christ is thus the perfect object of the Father's knowledge and love.

Through Christ, the Father reveals Himself to us in creation, providence and redemption. Scripture teaches that *"All things came into being through Him, and apart from Him nothing came into being that has come into being. In Him was life, and the life was the Light of men"* (Jn. 1:3-4).

Even before the incarnation of Christ, He was the true Light for every man coming into the world (John 1:9). All of the revelations of God in the Old Testament were mediated by Christ who alone *"...is the radiance of His glory and the exact representation of His nature"* (Hebrews 1:3).

When Abraham saw God, he saw Christ (John 8:56). When Isaiah saw the Lord sitting on the throne, he saw Christ (Isaiah 6:1; John 12:41). The Rock that sustained Israel

> *But by His doing you are in Christ Jesus, who became to us wisdom from God...*
> **– 1 Corinthians 1:30**

throughout their wanderings in the desert wilderness was none other than Christ Himself (1 Corinthians 10:4).

When the prophets spoke, it was by the Spirit of Christ (1 Pet. 1:10-12). Before Christ preached the Sermon on the Mount, He thundered from Mount Sinai, for Christ is the embodiment of law (Rom. 10:4) and its giver (James 4:12).

Since they are one in essence, Christ explains the Father (Jn. 1:18). Christ said "*...He who has seen Me has seen the Father; how can you say, 'Show us the Father'?*" (Jn. 14:9).

All knowledge of God comes to us in Christ. Paul wrote "*By common confession, great is the mystery of godliness: He who was revealed in the flesh, Was vindicated in the Spirit, Seen by angels, Proclaimed among the nations, Believed on in the world, Taken up in glory*" (1 Tim. 3:16).

The Cross of Christ is the most important revelation in all of history. On the Cross, Christ revealed God's abhorrence of sin, for sin must be condemned as it is the opposite of His holy nature. On the Cross, Christ revealed God's amazing love for humanity, for we are made in His own image. Christ saved us not by ignoring God's holy demands, but in taking them up and perfectly satisfying them for us (1 John 3:5). The Cross of Christ is thus the summary of God's wisdom to men, provided at His infinite cost for us to receive or reject. We would know nothing of God but for the wisdom of Christ.

> *Bible verse for devotion:*
>
> **Col. 2:2-3**–What is true knowledge of God's mystery?

Chapter 28

United to Christ who is our Righteousness

We are united to Christ who is our righteousness. The removal of our guilt and the restoration of God's favor comes only through union with Christ our Savior.

- Christ is the only revealer of the Father's righteousness.
- Apart from Christ, we would only receive condemnation.
- Apart from Christ, we would not know pardon and favor.

Christ is not only called the Word of God, but is also called "The LORD our righteousness". Scripture says that the Messiah would be "...*a righteous Branch...*" who would "...*do justice and righteousness...*" and "...*will be called, 'The LORD our righteousness'*" (Jeremiah 23:5-6).

Christ is the source and standard of right. He is perfect purity revealed, the exact image of God who alone is Holy.

Holiness is God's declaration and willing of His own infinite moral perfection and purity. Holiness is God's chief attribute and thus it is our highest motive and chief end.

God declares His holiness in righteousness and justice. God's righteousness requires our conformity to His moral perfection. In righteousness, God reveals His love of right. God's justice visits non-conformity to His perfection with penalty. In justice, God reveals His hatred of sin.

Psalm 97:2 states that "...*Righteousness and justice are the foundation of His throne.*" Of Christ it is therefore said "*YOUR THRONE, O GOD, IS FOREVER AND EVER...YOU HAVE LOVED RIGHTEOUSNESS AND HATED LAWLESSNESS...*" (Heb. 1:8-9).

God wills His holiness by His commands. In 1 Peter 1:16, God commands us to *"Be holy"*, where the ground of obligation is simply *"for I am holy."* This is God's self-willing.

> *But by His doing you are in Christ Jesus, who became to us wisdom from God, and righteousness...*
> **– 1 Corinthians 1:30**

Christ walked the earth in perfect righteousness all His days because He perfectly conforms to the holy will of God. Coming into the world, Christ said *"...Behold, I come; In the scroll of the book it is written of me. I delight to do Your will, O my God; Your Law is within my heart"* (Ps. 40:7-8; Heb. 10:5-10).

God restores us to favor in Christ for *"He made Him who knew no sin to be sin on our behalf, so that we might become the righteousness of God in Him"* (2 Cor. 5:21).

We are not merely declared to be righteous. We actually share in Christ's righteousness *"because we are members of His body"* (Eph. 5:30). We *"...were baptized into Christ..."* (Gal. 3:27). We are truly righteous for we are truly in Christ.

When Christ joined Himself to humanity, all the great exposures and liabilities of humanity fell upon Him. Christ took on our nature so that the whole mass and weight of God's holy displeasure against us would instead crush Him. Though personally pure, He was made sin for those united to Him through faith. His infinite suffering on the cross was an enduring of the reaction of God's holiness against sin and so was a bearing of penalty (Isa. 53:6; Gal. 3:13). For the very reason of His humanity, Christ bore in His own person all the guilt of humanity and is *"...the Lamb of God who..."* takes, and so *"...takes away the sin of the World"* (Jn. 1:29).

Bible verses for devotion:

Rev. 15:3-4–Do you sing the song of the Lamb?

Chapter 29

United to Christ who is our Sanctification

We are united to Christ who is our sanctification. The consecration of ourselves to God and the restoration of His image comes only through union with Christ.

- To be sanctified means to be set apart and made holy.
- Christ sets us apart by uniting Himself to us by His Spirit.
- Christ continuously makes us like Himself by His Spirit.

Christ is not only called 'The LORD our righteousness', but is also called "He who sanctifies". Scripture says "*For both He who sanctifies and those who are sanctified are all from one Father; for which reason He is not ashamed to call them brethren*" (Hebrews 2:11).

We are united to Christ who is the Messiah, the Holy One of God. We are set apart in Christ to share His union with the Father. We are thus Christ's brethren and God is our Father.

In union with Christ, we are given His righteousness and are therefore justified in God's holy presence. Guilt, which is the objective result of sin (Rom. 3:19), is removed once we are united to Christ so that we have no condemnation. In this sense, we are already sanctified (Acts 26:18). We are in Christ and thus consecrated to the Father by the Holy Spirit.

There is another sense in which we are presently being sanctified or made holy continually by Christ's Spirit. When we are united to Christ, the Holy Spirit gives us a new heart. Sanctification is the ongoing operation of the Spirit of Christ where this holy disposition is maintained and strengthened.

While all believers are free from guilt (Rom. 8:1), we are not yet free from depravity (Rom. 7:23). Depravity is the pollution resulting from sin. Sin has corrupted our will and affections. While we are indeed made new in Christ, we still

> *But by His doing you are in Christ Jesus, who became to us wisdom from God, and righteousness and sanctification...*
> — **1 Corinthians 1:30**

contend with tendencies to evil which last throughout life (Rom. 7; Gal. 5:17). Once we are united to Christ, He begins to repair this damage and restore His image in us (Phil. 1:16).

This is illustrated in each of the figures of our union with Christ. As Christ is our cornerstone and we are in permanent connection to Him, we are "...*growing into a holy temple in the Lord*" (Eph. 2:20). As Christ is the Husband of His church, He will "...*present to Himself the church in all her glory, having no spot or wrinkle or any such thing; but that she would be holy and blameless* (Eph. 5:27). As Christ is the Vine, He continually imparts His life to us as His branches so that we "...*bear much fruit...*" (John 15:8). As Christ is the head and we are His body, He "...*nourishes and cherishes it...because we are members of His body*" (Eph 5:29-30). As Christ is the Last Adam, He is the fount of a new humanity where He communicates to us His perfect humanity by faith so we "...*may have life, and have it abundantly*" (Jn. 10:10).

Christ sanctifies us by interpenetrating and energizing us with His Spirit who renews our mind and heart by the Word. He enables us to be more Christ-like by growing our faith and thus we progressively conquer our flesh (Rom. 8:13-14). Our sanctification is guaranteed, for "*Faithful is He who calls you, and He also will bring it to pass*" (1 Thess. 5:24).

Bible verse for devotion:

Jude 24-25– Is God able to present you faultless?

Chapter 30

United to Christ who is our Redemption

We are united to Christ who is our redemption. Our complete redemption, body and soul is only possible because we are united to Christ our Redeemer.

- In union with our Redeemer, Christ has redeemed us.
- In union with our Redeemer, Christ is redeeming us.
- In union with our Redeemer, Christ will redeem us.

Isaiah prophesied that *"A Redeemer will come..."* to save God's people. (Isa. 59:20). Paul declared this Redeemer to be Jesus Christ who *"...WILL REMOVE UNGODLINESS..."* and *"...TAKE AWAY THEIR SINS..."* (Rom. 11:26-27).

The redemption that Christ provides is past (Heb. 9:12), present (Heb. 9:14) and future (Heb 9:15). Justification is a past fact, sanctification is a present process and resurrection and glory are a future consummation (Titus 2:11-14).

In union with Christ, we are redeemed from ignorance by Christ who is our Wisdom (John 1:14). Christ our Prophet revealed God in grace and truth so that we might know God.

In union with Christ, we are redeemed from the curse of the Law by Him who is our Righteousness (Gal. 3:13). Christ our Priest bore our curse so we could be justified before God, restored to favor and set apart for His glory.

In union with Christ, we are being redeemed from the pollution of sin by Christ our Sanctification. Christ our King pours out His Spirit on us to rule our hearts, give us victory over sin, and transform us into His holy image (Rom. 5:17).

In union with Christ, we live for our Redeemer's glory *"knowing that you were not redeemed with perishable things like silver or gold from your futile way of life inherited from your forefathers, but with precious blood, as of a lamb unblemished and spotless, the blood of Christ"* (1 Pet. 1:18-19).

> *But by His doing you are in Christ Jesus, who became to us wisdom from God, and righteousness and sanctification and redemption.*
> **– 1 Corinthians 1:30**

In union with Christ, we anticipate the completion of our redemption. Christ the King will deliver our bodies from the grave and into His courts above. Paul expressed this hope, saying that *"...having the first fruits of the Spirit, even we ourselves groan within ourselves, waiting eagerly for our adoption as sons, the redemption of our body"* (Rom. 8:23).

Our earthly bodies are dying and suffer much. Although we possess *"...a perishable body..."* that is *"...sown in dishonor..."*, and *"...in weakness..."* and as *"...a natural body..."*, it will truly be *"....raised an imperishable body..."*, *"...raised in glory..."*, *"...raised in power..."*, for *"...it is raised a spiritual body..."* united to Christ (1 Cor. 15:42-44).

Our final redemption will involve deliverance from all death, sorrow, and pain (Rev. 21:4), deliverance from fallen surroundings (Rev. 21:1), as well as from the remains of evil in our hearts (Rev. 21:5). We will enter Heaven, free from sin (Rev. 21:27), free from curse (Rev. 22:3) and darkness (Rev. 22:5). We will be completely delivered from all evil. Our body and soul will be brought together fully perfected into blissful communion with Christ, forever sharing His reign and glory.

Bible verses for devotion:

Eph. 4:30–Are you sealed for the day of Redemption?

VI. TOGETHER WITH CHRIST: TEN IDENTIFICATIONS OF EVERY CHRISTIAN

Chapter 31

Crucified Together with Christ

*In His crucifixion, Christ redeemed us from the curse
of the law and reconciled us to God. In our crucifixion
with Christ, we escape sin's penalty.*

- In Christ's crucifixion, Christ was cursed by God's law.
- In Christ's crucifixion, He gave Himself in grace and love.
- In Christ's crucifixion, we are redeemed from sin's curse.

Paul declares that believers "...*have been crucified with Christ...*" (Gal. 2:20). Our union with Christ is so close that His suffering on the cross is counted on our behalf. It is as if we were crucified together with Him and suffered the curse. Crucifixion with Christ is key to understanding redemption.

The whole race was shut out from God by its sin. David asked in Psalm 24:3 *"Who may ascend into the hill of the LORD? And who may stand in His holy place?"* As the fundamental attribute of God is holiness, which is His self-affirming perfect purity, God requires righteousness in us.

All sin is an offense against God. Sin is an act or state of opposition to His will which has for its effect God's personal wrath (John 3:18, 36). Sin, as antagonism to God's holy will, involves guilt. This guilt, or obligation to satisfy the outraged holiness of God, is described in terms of "debtor" and "debt" (Matt. 6:12; Matt. 18:27; Luke 11:4; Rom. 6:23; Col. 2:14).

Although God's righteousness condemns sin, His love provides the remedy to sin's penalty by way of substitution. Christ was cursed for us to meet the holy demands of the law.

Gal. 3:13-14 says *"Christ redeemed us from the curse of the Law, having become a curse for us—for it is written, "CURSED IS EVERYONE WHO HANGS ON A TREE"— in order that in Christ Jesus the blessing of Abraham might come to the Gentiles,*

> *I have been crucified with Christ; and it is no longer I who live, but Christ lives in me; and the life which I now live in the flesh I live by faith in the Son of God, who loved me and gave Himself up for me. I do not nullify the grace of God, for if righteousness comes through the Law, then Christ died needlessly.*
> **–Galatians 2:20-21**

so that we would receive the promise of the Spirit through faith." Christ was cursed so that we may receive God's favor.

This substitution is unknown to mere law, and above and beyond the powers of law. It is an operation of grace. Grace, however, does not violate or suspend law, but takes it up into itself and fulfills it. Christ was both our Judge and our Sin-bearer. The righteousness of law was maintained in that the Source of all law perfectly fulfilled its demands (Rom. 10:4).

Rom. 8:3 says *"For what the law could not do, weak as it was through the flesh, God did: sending His own Son in the likeness of sinful flesh and as an offering for sin, He condemned sin in the flesh."* God did this by sending His Son in a nature which in us is identified with sin. In connection with sin, and as an offering for sin, God condemned sin, by condemning Christ. We are accepted in Christ (Eph. 1:6).

We were crucified with Christ (Gal. 2:20). God's holiness is satisfied. We are redeemed and reconciled (Rom. 5:6-11).

Bible verses for devotion:

Romans 8:3-4– How is the law fully satisfied in us?

Chapter 32

Died Together with Christ

In His death, Christ released us from the dominion of sin by destroying its power over us. In our death with Christ, we escape sin's power.

- In His death, the condemning power of sin is destroyed.
- In His death, the enslaving power of sin is destroyed.
- In His death, the killing power of sin is destroyed.

Scripture says that believers *"...have died with Christ..."* (Col. 2:20). Our union with Christ is so near that His death is considered to be our own. It is as if we died together with Him so that we would be dead to sin and free from its power. Death with Christ is key to understanding our deliverance.

After a long discourse on how we have died together with Christ, Paul says *"Therefore there is now no condemnation for those who are in Christ Jesus"* (Rom. 8:1). In our death with Christ, we are set free from sin's condemning power.

All men are condemned by sin (Rom. 5:18). No person or class can escape, for we *"...are all under sin..."* (Rom. 3:9).

The remedy is His taking *"...our sins in His body on the cross, so that we might die to sin and live to righteousness; for by His wounds you were healed"* (1 Pet. 2:24).

This means that our sins have been removed from us. Sin can no longer condemn us because Christ has taken our sins. When sin comes looking to condemn us, we are far gone and can't be found because the dead can't be pursued. In our death with Christ, the condemning power of sin is destroyed.

In our death with Christ, we are set "...*free from the law of sin*..."(Rom 8:2).

We were all enslaved by sin. Sin made us "...*slaves to impurity and to lawlessness, resulting in further lawlessness*..." (Rom. 6:19). We could not break its chains.

> *Therefore there is now no condemnation for those who are in Christ Jesus. For the law of the Spirit of life in Christ Jesus has set you free from the law of sin and of death.*
> —Romans 8:1-2

The remedy is "*that our old self was crucified with Him, in order that our body of sin might be done away with, so that we would no longer be slaves to sin; for he who has died is freed from sin*" (Rom. 6:6-7). Sin is now powerless to control us. We have "...*been freed from sin*..." so that we can now become "...*slaves of righteousness*" (Rom. 6:18). In our death with Christ, the enslaving power of sin is destroyed.

In our death with Christ, we are set "...*free from...death*" (Rom 8:2). It is by Christ's death that we have eternal life.

We were all said to be "...*dead in your trespasses and sins*" (Eph. 2:1). We were spiritually dead to God, separated from His favor, and deserving of everlasting death as the reward of sin, "*For the wages of sin is death*..." (Rom. 6:23).

The remedy is in "...*our Savior Christ Jesus, who abolished death and brought life and immortality to light through the gospel*" (2 Tim. 1:10). Death is brought down by Christ. Death's sting is removed as it now gives way to life. Death and the devil are made powerless (Heb. 2:14-15). In our death with Christ, the killing power of sin is destroyed.

United with Christ, we escape sin's power by His death.

Bible verses for devotion:

2 Cor. 5:14-15– In light of His death, how do we live?

Chapter 33

Buried Together with Christ

In His burial, Christ's atonement is declared as finished and sufficient. Buried with Him, we are hidden from sin and God remembers our sins no more. Buried with Christ, we are forever free in Him.

- His burial is the recognition of His work as finished.
- His burial is the recognition of His work as fixed.
- His burial is the removal of ourselves from sin's domain.
- His burial is the removal of our sins from God's sight.

Scripture states that we have "...*been buried with Him...*" (Col. 2:12). Our union with Christ is so strong that His burial is considered to be our own. It is as if we're buried together with Him so that we could forever rest in the Prince of Peace. Burial with Christ is key to understanding His finished work.

Burial is the act of placing a dead person in the grave. It is as official recognition that one's course of life is complete. The dead are "...*lain down...*" and "...*at rest*" (Job 3:13). They are spoken of as having their days fulfilled (Job 14:6). Buried in Christ, believers "...*rest from their labors...*" (Rev. 14:13).

When Christ was laid and sealed in the tomb, it was a recognition of His completed work for which He was sent to accomplish. On the cross, "...*He said, "It is finished!" And He bowed His head and gave up His spirit*" (John 19:30).

Our burial with Christ testifies that His saving work for us is complete. It is finished. Buried together, we rest from our works just as He rested from His works (Hebrews 4:10).

Burial is a fixed state for us (Job 7:9-10). We can't bring back or restore those we bury.

Our burial with Christ testifies that in His death, our sin and death have been dealt with once and for all. Christ "...*offered*

> *Therefore we have been buried with Him through baptism into death, so that as Christ was raised from the dead through the glory of the Father, so we too might walk in newness of life.*
> **—Romans 6:4**

one sacrifice for sins for all time..." (Heb. 10:12). Christ "...*died for sins once for all, the just for the unjust, so that He might bring us to God...*" (1 Pet. 3:18).

His work is perfectly sufficient. It never needs repeating (Heb. 7:27). The power and penalty of sin can't be restored. Buried together with Him, we are forever reconciled to God.

Burial is a separation of the body from perception. Those whom we bury are removed and hid from sight (Gen. 23:4).

Our burial with Christ testifies that we are forever removed from sin's domain. Our God has "...*rescued us from the domain of darkness, and transferred us to the kingdom of His beloved Son*" (Col. 1:13). Buried with Him, we have triumphed over the dominion of darkness (Col. 2:14-15).

Our burial with Christ testifies that our sins are forever removed from God's sight. Our sin is thrown behind His back, into the depths of the sea, and as far the east is from the west (Is. 38:17; Mi. 7:19; Ps. 103:12). God has promised "...*I will remember their sins no more*" (Heb. 8:12; 10:17).

Buried with Christ, we are forever in Him. "*For you have died and your life is hidden with Christ in God*" (Col. 3:3).

> **Bible verses for devotion:**
> **Jn. 8:34-36**—How are we made forever free?

Chapter 34

Quickened Together with Christ

In His resurrection, we are made alive together with Christ. Christ makes us to be a new creation in Him. Our new life is Christ living His life in us by His Spirit.

- Quickened together, we are made to be spiritually alive.
- Quickened together, we are made new creatures.
- Quickened together, Christ lives His life in ours.

Scripture states that we have been made *"...alive together with Him..."* (Col. 2:13). Our union with Christ is so vital that the quickening of His body is considered to be ours. It is as if we're made alive together with Him in the grave so that we could receive life from the True Vine. Being made alive with Christ is key to understanding our regeneration.

Apart from Christ, all men are declared to be *"...dead in your trespasses and sins"* (Eph. 2:1). The spiritually dead walk in futility *"being darkened in their understanding, excluded from the life of God because of the ignorance that is in them, because of the hardness of their heart"* (Eph. 4:18). Being dead to God, unbelievers are enslaved to all that is contrary to His holiness. They *"...having become callous, have given themselves over to sensuality for the practice of every kind of impurity with greediness"* (Eph. 4:19).

In Christ's resurrection, we now live to God, *"For just as the Father raises the dead and gives them life, even so the Son also gives life to whom He wishes"* (John 5:21). Christ promised *"...because I live, you will live also"* (John 14:19).

Having died with Christ, we are made alive together with Him. We are now fully immersed in Him whose life is the very ground and principle of our being. We now partake of Christ so that His life dominates ours and manifests itself through us.

> *But God, being rich in mercy, because of His great love with which He loved us, even when we were dead in our transgressions, made us alive together with Christ (by grace you have been saved).*
> —**Ephesians 2:4-5**

Our baptism into Christ is the outward picture of the inward immersion of our soul into His very life. In Christ, we become new creatures. Scripture says *"Therefore if anyone is in Christ, he is a new creature; the old things passed away; behold, new things have come"* (2 Cor. 5:17). We are no more in Adam, but are now in Christ. Our ruling disposition which before was sinful, is now holy. We are free to live for Christ.

The Lord's Supper is the outward picture of the inward receiving of Christ's life into our own. The wine is the symbol of Christ's death, but it is by His death that we live. Just as broken bread sustains our life, Christ's broken body sustains our soul. This continuous impartation of life leads us to say *"...it is no longer I who live, but Christ lives in me..."* (Gal. 2:20). This divine interpenetration and energizing of the soul is the life of Christ being lived through us by the Holy Spirit.

The resurrected Christ breathed on His disciples saying *"Receive the Holy Spirit"* (Jn. 20:22). This anticipated the sending of His Spirit to forever dwell in us. Quickened with Christ, we are infinitely closer with God than when man first *"...became a living being"* by His original breath (Gen. 2:7).

Bible verses for devotion:

1 Cor. 15:45 —How is Christ a life-giving spirit?

Chapter 35

Raised Together with Christ

In Christ's resurrection, we are raised together out of the grave to live in Christ. Raised together, we are accepted by God and called to walk in Christlikeness.

- Raised together, we are freed from death to live in Christ.
- Raised together, we are given the righteousness of Christ.
- Raised together, we begin to be made holy by Christ.

Scripture states that God "...*raised us up with Him...*" (Eph. 2:6). Our union with Christ is so absolute that His raising is considered to be our own. It is as if we're raised up together with Him from the grave so that we could have eternal life and God's approval in Christ. Being raised with Christ is key to grasping justification and sanctification.

Christ's resurrection turned the grave into a scene of life. The tomb was no longer closed, but was open. Christ's linen wraps were left behind. His face-cloth was carefully rolled up and set aside. Two angels in dazzling appearance sat in the grave, one at the head and one at the feet where the body of Jesus had been lying. The angels recognized the disciple's perplexity, fear and alarm and brought comfort to them with good news saying "*Why do you seek the living One among the dead? He is not here, but He has risen...*" (Luke 24:5-6).

In raising Christ from the dead, God put "*....an end to the agony of death, since it was impossible for Him to be held in its power*" (Acts 2:24). Raised with Christ, we forever live, for He said "*...Unbind him, and let him go*" (Jn. 11:44).

Christ's death and resurrection must be linked together in our redemption. His death is ours and so too is His life. Christ "...*was delivered over because of our transgressions,*

> *Having been buried with Him in baptism, in which you were also raised up with Him through faith in the working of God, who raised Him from the dead.*
> —Colossians 2:12

and was raised because of our justification" (Romans 4:25).

By His finished work on the cross, Christ fulfilled all righteousness. Once the law's demands were satisfied, He could not be held under its curse. To remain in the grave would turn law into lawlessness and glory into shame. The resurrection of Christ proved that God's justice was satisfied.

Raised together, we are justified and given favor with God. Raised with Him, "...*He has now reconciled you in His fleshly body through death, in order to present you before Him holy and blameless and beyond reproach*" (Col. 1:22).

Raised together with Christ, we begin to be made holy by Christ. Christ makes us to be what He has already bestowed on us. This is the beginning of our sanctification in which we are conformed to Christ by His word and Spirit (John 14:26).

A broken ship is brought into port and secured to the dock. She is safe, but not sound. Repairs may take time. We are made safe by justification and sound by sanctification.

We are assured that "...*God has not only raised the Lord, but will also raise us up through His power*" (1 Cor. 6:14). Raised together with Christ, the dead come to life, the guilty are justified, and sinners are made holy and thus Christlike.

Bible verses for devotion:

Jude 24-25 —How do we stand before God?

Chapter 36

Seated Together with Christ

In Christ's ascension, we are seated together with Christ in heaven. Seated together, we are crowned with glory and honor and reign triumphantly in Christ.

- Seated together with Christ, we are exalted in Christ.
- Seated together with Christ, we are blessed in Christ.
- Seated together with Christ, we reign as victors in Christ.

Scripture states that God "...*seated us with Him in the heavenly places...*" (Eph. 2:6). Our union with Christ is so complete that His exaltation and enthronement is considered to be our own. It is as if we're seated together with Him in his ascension so that we could be exalted and reign victoriously. Being seated with Him is key to living triumphantly in Him.

When Christ fulfilled all righteousness, "...*He sat down at the right hand of the Majesty on high*" (Heb. 1:3). Christ is now "...*crowned with glory and honor...*" (Heb. 2:9). We honor and obey Him for "*He is the one whom God exalted to His right hand as a Prince and a Savior...*" (Acts 5:31).

Christ who once "...*humbled Himself...*" is now "...*highly exalted...*" (Phil. 2:8-9). Christ's glory that He shared with the Father from all eternity is now on full display (Jn. 17:5).

Having received Christ through faith, believers are now seated with Christ in the heavenly places (Eph. 2:6). His holy favor, glory, honor, and divine right is counted as our own. Seeing us as seated in Him, Christ has said "*The glory which You have given Me I have given to them...*" (John 17:22).

Christ, who is our glorified Head, shares His blessed state with us who are seated with Him as His own body. He is exalted to show "...*the surpassing riches of His grace in kindness toward us in Christ Jesus*" (Eph. 2:7). We thus receive "...*every spiritual blessing in the heavenly places in Christ*" (Eph. 1:3).

These gracious spiritual blessings describe the receiving

> *But God, being rich in mercy, because of His great love with which He loved us, even when we were dead in our transgressions, made us alive together with Christ (by grace you have been saved), and raised us up with Him, and seated us with Him in the heavenly places in Christ Jesus, so that in the ages to come He might show the surpassing riches of His grace in kindness toward us in Christ Jesus.*
> *–Ephesians 2:4-7*

of Christ Himself. There is no higher blessing. The psalmist, rightly proclaimed, "...*In Your presence is fullness of joy; In Your right hand there are pleasures forever*" (Psalm 16:11).

The Father has exalted Christ and "...*put all things in subjection under His feet, and gave Him as head over all things to the church...*" (Eph. 1:22). His reign at the Father's right hand includes both the procession of the Holy Spirit by which the church was formed to be His body (Acts 2:33; 1 Cor. 12:13) and His intercession for His body (Rom. 8:34).

Seated with Christ in the heavenly realm, we reign with Him as victors over sin and death. We who have received "...*the abundance of grace and of the gift of righteousness will reign in life through the One, Jesus Christ*" (Rom. 5:17).

Bible verses for devotion:

Revelation 1:5-6–What has Christ made us to be?

Chapter 37

Working Together with Christ

We are co-laborers with Christ in proclaiming the good news of salvation in Jesus Christ. Salvation is truly His work, but He employs us to call men to Him.

- Christ works with us and in us to accomplish His work.
- We are prepared and empowered by Christ for His work.
- We work to proclaim Christ and present all men in Him.
- Christ's co-labors so closely with us that our work is His.

Scripture states that we are "*...working together with Him...*" (2 Cor. 6:1). Our union with Christ is so entwined that He who reconciled us to God has given us His ministry of reconciliation (2 Cor. 5:18-21). Christ is making an appeal through us to all men to be reconciled to God. Working together with Christ is key to being His faithful ambassador.

Before His ascension, Christ commissioned His disciples saying "*All authority has been given to Me in heaven and on earth. Go therefore and make disciples of all the nations, baptizing them in the name of the Father and the Son and the Holy Spirit, teaching them to observe all that I commanded you; and lo, I am with you always, even to the end of the age*" (Matt. 28:18-20).

Christ's command to "*Go therefore and make disciples*" is inseparable from both His complete authority over all things and His sure promise that "*I am with you always*". Thus, as the church proclaimed that Christ is risen, it is said that "*...the Lord worked with them...*" (Mk. 16:20, Acts 14:3).

The writer of Hebrews says that the church acted as Christ's ambassadors in declaring His great salvation which He had first delcared. In their faithful witness, God was "...*also testifying with them...*" (Heb. 2:4). This is why Paul could write that "...*we are God's fellow workers...*" (1 Cor. 3:9).

> *So Jesus said to them again, "Peace be with you; as the Father has sent Me, I also send you." And when He had said this, He breathed on them and said to them, "Receive the Holy Spirit.*
> **–John 20:21-22**

Believers have been prepared for the work for which they were comissioned for in Christ. Scripture says "*For we are His workmanship, created in Christ Jesus for good works, which God prepared beforehand so that we would walk in them*" (Eph. 2:10). God perfectly fashioned us in Christ and ordained our steps so we would be His vessels for His work.

Our Lord Jesus declared "*You did not choose Me but I chose you, and appointed you that you would go and bear fruit, and that your fruit would remain...*" (John 15:16).

Christ who appointed us for His work of reconciliation, empowers us to accomplish it. Paul said "*We proclaim Him, admonishing every man and teaching every man with all wisdom, so that we may present every man complete in Christ. For this purpose also I labor, striving according to His power, which mightily works within me* (Col. 1:28-29).

We are so at one with Christ that our proclamation is called His own, for we are said to "...*have been speaking in Christ...*" (2 Cor. 12:19). Likewise, His proclamation is called ours, for it is "...*Christ who speaks in me...*" (2 Cor. 13:3).

Bible verses for devotion:

Jn. 14:12-14–How do we work together with Christ?

Chapter 38

Suffering Together with Christ

We suffer together with Christ in conforming to His image and living for His sake. Christ is with us in our sufferings and works them for our good and His glory.

- We suffer together by growing in conformity to Christ.
- We suffer together by living for Christ's cause and sake.
- We suffer together by Christ's assistance and direction.

Scripture states that "*...we suffer with Him ...*" (Rom. 8:17). Our union with Christ is so inseparable that He who bore our griefs and carried our sorrows (Is. 53:4) grants us "*...not only to believe in Him, but also to suffer for His sake*" (Phil. 1:29). As Christ's suffering led to glory, so too will ours. Suffering with Christ is key to living for Him and His glory.

We suffer together with Christ by growing in conformity to Christ. Jesus said "*I am the true vine, and My Father is the vinedresser. Every branch in Me that does not bear fruit, He takes away; and every branch that bears fruit, He prunes it so that it may bear more fruit*" (Jn. 15:1-2). If you bear fruit in Christ, you will endure suffering under Divine superintendence that is necessary to bear more fruit for Him.

Coupled with the Vinedresser's cutting is the enmity and grief toward evil on our part that stems from our new life in Christ. Our new spiritual nature is at fierce war with our old sinful flesh. Paul wrote "*For the flesh sets its desire against the Spirit, and the Spirit against the flesh; for these are in opposition to one another...*" (Gal. 5:17). We would not know this bitter conflict apart from being a new creation in Christ.

Growing in conformity to the True Vine, every believer follows Christ in learning obedience in the same way (Hebrews 5:8) and being perfected by the same means (Hebrews 2:10). In this pattern, His sufferings truly become ours.

> *For just as the sufferings of Christ are ours in abundance, so also our comfort is abundant through Christ.*
> **–2 Corinthians 1:5**

We also suffer together with Christ in living for Him and for His sake. Jesus said "*...If anyone wishes to come after Me, he must deny himself, and take up his cross and follow Me*" (Matt. 16:24). To suffer in His cause and for His sake is to bear afflictions as He did and be persecuted in like manner by the world. This shows that we are truly united to Christ.

Christ speaks of our suffering together with Himself under the figures of drinking His cup and being baptized with His baptism (Mark 10:38). Likewise, Paul spoke of our being planted together in the likeness of Christ's death (Rom. 6:5) and being crucified to the world by Christ's cross (Gal. 6:14). As His body (1 Cor. 12:27), we are "*always carrying about in the body the dying of Jesus, so that the life of Jesus also may be manifested in our body*" (2 Corinthians 4:10).

United to Christ, we have the peace "*...that we have been destined for this*" (1 Thess. 3:3) and "*...suffer according to the will of God...*" (1 Pet. 4:19) who "*...causes all things to work together for good to those who love God, to those who are called according to His purpose*" (Rom. 8:28).

We can say "*Now I rejoice in my sufferings...in filling up what is lacking in Christ's afflictions*" (Col. 1:24) as every suffering reduces the number and hastens His glorious day.

Bible verses for devotion:

Acts 9:1-5 –Was Saul persecuting our risen Lord?

Chapter 39

Heirs together with Christ

We are heirs together with Christ. In Christ, we have been made children of God by His Spirit. We are thus given the same inheritance that is due to Christ.

- We are made sons of God through union with God's Son.
- Christ our Elder Brother shares His inheritance with us.
- As fellow heirs with Christ, we receive God as our portion.

Scripture states that we are "...*fellow heirs with Christ*..." (Rom. 8:17). Our union with Christ is so wondrous that He who is the "...*heir of all things*..." (Heb. 1:2) shares His great inheritance with us. Through His Spirit, Christ imparts the very life of God to us. As joint heirs with Christ, all that is His becomes ours also. In Christ, we inherit the gracious gift of life and eternal glory which is our forever dwelling with God.

John teaches that we become God's children by being born of God. When we are quickened by Christ, He imparts His life to us and we are "...*born of the Spirit*" (Jn. 3:8). We know that "...*as many as received Him, to them He gave the right to become children of God, even to those who believe in His name, who were born, not of blood nor of the will of the flesh nor of the will of man, but of God*" (Jn. 1:12-13).

Where John uses the figure of birth to describe how we become children of God, Paul uses the figure of adoption. Paul teaches that "*He predestined us to adoption as sons through Jesus Christ to Himself, according to the kind intention of His will, to the praise of the glory of His grace, which He freely bestowed on us in the Beloved*" (Eph. 1:5-6).

Born of God and adopted by God, we are made to be God's sons only in union with His perfect Son. Christ is therefore the "...the *firstborn among many brethren*" (Rom. 8:29). Christ and His church are said to be "...*all from one Father; for which reason He is not ashamed to call them brethren*" (Heb. 2:11).

> *And if children, heirs also, heirs of God and fellow heirs with Christ, if indeed we suffer with Him so that we may also be glorified with Him.*
> —Romans 8:17

To be fellow heirs with Christ is breathtaking. Consider how "...*in Him all the fullness of Deity dwells in bodily form, and in Him you have been made complete...*" (Col. 2:9-10). All that Christ is and has is given to us in union with Him (Jn. 1:16). Hence "...*all things belong to you, and you belong to Christ; and Christ belongs to God.*" (1 Cor. 3:22-23).

Our inheritance surpasses any conceivable blessing, for God Himself is our portion and our lot. We adoringly sing *"The LORD is the portion of my inheritance and my cup; You support my lot. The lines have fallen to me in pleasant places; Indeed, my heritage is beautiful to me"* (Ps. 16:5-6).

Our birthright and heritage in Christ is fully the perfect love of the Father for the Son. As we are in Christ, we hear the Father say "...*You are My beloved Son, in You I am well-pleased*" (Luke 3:22). This love led John to exclaim *"See how great a love the Father has bestowed on us, that we would be called children of God; and such we are..."* (1 John 3:1).

As heirs together with Christ, we have obtained "...*an inheritance which is imperishable and undefiled and will not fade away, reserved in heaven for you*" (1 Peter 3:4).

Bible verses for devotion:

Eph. 1:13-14 –Is our inheritance present or future?

Chapter 40

Glorified Together in Christ

In His heavenly ascension, the glory of Christ was unveiled. In heaven, the glory of God in Christ will be revealed to and in us. We will behold His face forever.

- Glorified together, we will see the glory of God in Christ.
- Glorified together, we will be changed into His likeness.
- Glorified together, we will fellowship with Christ forever.

Scripture states that we will be *"...glorified with Him"* (Rom. 8:17). Our union with Christ is so consummate that the *"...the bright morning star"* (Rev. 22:16) will reveal His own glory in us (Rev. 2:28). Just as we are presently seated together with Christ in His exaltation and enthronement, we will one day be in His gloriously revealed presence in heaven possessing *"...the unfading crown of glory"* (1 Peter 5:4).

The Father's glory is the vast sum of all His attributes. His glory is so great that Paul says that the Father *"...dwells in unapproachable light, whom no man has seen or can see..."* (1 Tim. 6:16). John likewise writes that *"No one has seen God at any time; the only begotten God who is in the bosom of the Father, He has explained Him"* (John 1:18).

We see God's glory through Christ who *"...is the radiance of His glory and the exact representation of His nature..."* (Heb. 1:3). Just as Christ mediates all knowledge of God here (Matt. 11:27; 2 Cor. 4:6), it is likewise in heaven. In heaven we will see by the glory of God in Christ, *"...for the glory of God has illumined it, and its lamp is the Lamb"* (Rev. 21:23).

In heaven, *"we will be like Him, because we will see Him just as He is"* (1 John 3:2). We will be perfected into Christ's image, bearing as much of His glory as we can hold.

The Holy Spirit will perfect us not by acting on us from without, but by transforming us from within (Phil. 1:6). The Spirit who came down at Pentecost to form a spiritual body out of flesh, will at the Second Coming return to heaven in that body made like Christ's (Phil. 3:21).

> *And if children, heirs also, heirs of God and fellow heirs with Christ, if indeed we suffer with Him so that we may also be glorified with Him. For I consider that the sufferings of this present time are not worthy to be compared with the glory that is to be revealed to us. For the anxious longing of the creation waits eagerly for the revealing of the sons of God.*
> **—Romans 8:17-19**

We are promised that *"When Christ, who is our life, is revealed, then you also will be revealed with Him in glory"* (Col. 3:4). All of creation longs to see God's glory revealed in us at *"...the revealing of the sons of God"* (Romans 8:19).

When Christ faced His darkest hour, He longed for us to see His glory. He prayed, *"Father, I desire that they also, whom You have given Me, be with Me where I am, so that they may see My glory which You have given Me, for You loved Me before the foundation of the world"* (John 17:24).

Crucified together, died together, buried together, quickened together, raised together, seated together, working together, suffering together, heirs together and glorified together. How we long to see His beautiful face!

Bible verse for devotion:

Romans 8:30 —Why is "glorified" in the past tense?

Made in the USA
Monee, IL
04 November 2024

69343169R00062